Y0-CCE-091

Gretchen Bitterlin
Dennis Johnson
Donna Price
Sylvia Ramirez
K. Lynn Savage, Series Editor

Ventures

CIVICS WORKSHEETS

with **Lois Miller**

CAMBRIDGE
UNIVERSITY PRESS

CAMBRIDGE UNIVERSITY PRESS
Cambridge, New York, Melbourne, Madrid, Cape Town, Singapore,
São Paulo, Delhi, Dubai, Tokyo

Cambridge University Press
32 Avenue of the Americas, New York, NY 10013-2473, USA

www.cambridge.org
Information on this title: www.cambridgeorg/9780521135030

© Cambridge University Press 2010

This publication is in copyright. Subject to statutory exception
and to the provisions of relevant collective licensing agreements,
no reproduction of any part may take place without the written
permission of Cambridge University Press.

First published 2010

Printed in the United States of America

A catalog record for this publication is available from the British Library

ISBN 978-0-521-13503-0   Ventures Civics Worksheets

Cambridge University Press has no responsibility for the persistence or
accuracy of URLs for external or third-party Internet Web sites referred to in
this publication, and does not guarantee that any content on such Web sites is,
or will remain, accurate or appropriate. Information regarding prices, travel
timetables, and other factual information given in this work are correct at
the time of first printing, but Cambridge University Press does not guarantee
the accuracy of such information thereafter.

Art direction, book design, and layout services: Adventure House, NYC

....

It is normally necessary for written permission for copying to be obtained *in advance*
from a publisher. The worksheets in this book are designed to be copied and distributed in
class. The normal requirements are waived here and it is not necessary to write to
Cambridge University Press for permission for an individual teacher to make copies
for use within his or her own classroom. Only those pages which carry the wording
"© Cambridge University Press" may be copied.

Photo credits

Cover *(all)* ©Shutterstock
8 *(all)* ©Shutterstock
81 *(both)* ©Shutterstock

84 ©Shutterstock
86 ©Shutterstock
90 *(both)* ©Shutterstock

Illustration credits

John Batten: 21
Denny Bond: 22, 31
Chuck Gonzales: 26
Larry Jost: 57
Frank Montagna: 7

Jim Nuttle: 6, 47
Monika Roe: 3, 5, 20
William Waitzman: 4, 10, 11, 39
Mark Watkinson: 23

To the teacher

What are the *Ventures* Civics Worksheets?

The *Ventures* Civics Worksheets are designed to supplement coverage of civics in the *Ventures* series. These reproducible worksheets and the Teacher tips that follow will help your students become better informed and more active members of their communities.

Using the worksheets

Each worksheet addresses civics objectives at the low-beginning, high-beginning, and intermediate levels through a variety of activities involving document literacy, readings, dialogs, vocabulary development, crossword puzzles, and pair and group discussions. Consider each worksheet as an introduction to its corresponding objective in consumer economics, community resources, health, employment, or history and government. We recommend using each worksheet as a springboard for a longer lesson. In addition to the suggestions below, we have provided a list of Teacher tips on pages 91– 94 to give you worksheet-specific ideas for expansion.

The worksheets are meant to be used in conjunction with the *Ventures* series. See pages iv–v for the Table of Contents, which recommends when to integrate the civics worksheets into your teaching of the *Ventures* Student's Books. The *Ventures* Civics Worksheets are correlated to CASAS, Illinois Community College Board, and Florida civics objectives and guidelines. See pages vi–x for the Correlations chart.

Expanding the material

The *Ventures* Civics Worksheets are perfectly poised for expansion because each worksheet objective can function as the subject matter for any exercise, activity, or project that practices other skill-based objectives from the curriculum, such as listening, speaking, reading, and writing. With that in mind, here are some ways to expand upon the material.

Use authentic materials

Take advantage of the wealth of authentic materials available in your area. Pick up and bring to your classroom local restaurant menus, maps, bus and train schedules, health-center brochures, newspapers, photos, phone books, bank slips, employment applications, and sample leases or rental agreements. Using authentic materials exposes students to real language and cultural information.

Invite guest speakers

Change your classroom routine by inviting guest speakers from local businesses, community services, and government offices. For example, call a local community leader and explain that your ESL class is interested in learning more about the neighborhood and what he or she does. You can also request a visit from the fire or police departments. Guest speakers offer fresh perspectives and allow students to engage with members of the community.

Take a field trip

When time permits, take your students on a field trip. Post offices, libraries, and supermarkets are good options. For government themes, consider a guided tour of City Hall or local court facilities. Such trips can also be combined with a ride on public transportation to practice reading maps or a meal at an inexpensive restaurant to practice reading menus. It is important to arrange the trip in advance with the manager in charge of the site and to visit the site before the field trip, if possible. Prepare students for what they can expect to see and do. Pre-teach key vocabulary and distribute brochures, if applicable. Give clear directions if the class will meet directly at the site.

Integrate technology

Incorporate video clips from local news programs into your lessons. They often discuss community resources, elections, public transportation, and other relevant topics. Audio clips from the Internet can also provide students with information related to worksheet objectives while developing their English listening skills. Visit www.npr.org or a local radio station's Web site to locate topical audio recordings. Exposing your students to various forms of technology will enliven the classroom and create a more stimulating learning environment.

Explore the Web

In the computer lab or on their own, students can use *Ventures* Citizenship Arcade for free citizenship exam preparation. Go to www.cambridge.org/us/esl/venturesadulted/venturesarcade

Contents

Introduction

Intermediate Worksheets

Use with *Ventures* Student's Books 3 and 4

Additional Resources

Correlations

WORKSHEET	CIVICS OBJECTIVES / COMPETENCIES (CASAS/FL/IL)
1	**CASAS** (1) Identify, evaluate, and compare financial service options in the community such as banks, credit unions, check-cashing services, and credit cards.
2	**CASAS** (4) Describe methods and procedures to obtain housing and related services, including low-cost community housing.
3	**CASAS** (6) Identify basic housing issues, including home-maintenance problems, tenant rights, and responsibilities. Advocate for solutions.
	IL HO4. Report housing problems to landlords, property associations, or other officials. / HO5. Contact utility providers for service or to report a problem. / HO6. Identify resources for resolving housing problems.
4	**CASAS** (7) Identify effective ways to safeguard families and homes, including the use of community and governmental resources.
5	**CASAS** (8) Identify a local community need or civic-oriented complaint; research and address the issue.
	IL CR6. Participate in community outreach programs to enhance personal and community safety.
6	**CASAS** (10) Identify, locate, and map important places in the community, the state, and the country, and list services available and/or importance of each location.
7	**CASAS** (11) Research and describe the cultural backgrounds that reflect the local cross-cultural society and that may present a barrier to civic participation.
8	**CASAS** (12) Describe and access services offered at the DMV, and read, interpret, and identify regulations, roadside signs, and traffic signals.
	IL CR3. State the laws regarding safe transportation of themselves and their children in motor vehicles.
9	**CASAS** (13) Interact with educational institutions, including schools for children and schools or agencies with programs for adult learners.
10	**CASAS** (15) Demonstrate basic knowledge and awareness of the emergency services available in the community and ways to contact and use emergency services and legal-assistance agencies.
	IL CR1. Call 911 or other police/fire emergency telephone numbers to report an emergency.
	FL Collect and share information with other students on emergency services in the community.
11	**CASAS** (16) Follow appropriate procedures to access community-assistance agencies available in the case of an emergency or disaster.
	IL CR2. Distinguish between emergency and nonemergency situations.
12	**CASAS** (17) Analyze community resources in order to access appropriate assistance and/or find appropriate ways to prevent or solve family and/or community problems such as substance abuse, spousal abuse, and gang violence.
	IL HE6. Identify community resources for crisis services, including domestic violence, child abuse, and substance abuse.
13	**CASAS** (18) Access services in the community available to seniors.
14	**CASAS** (19) Identify the rights of immigrants in the United States, and access local and state agencies that specialize in these rights.

CASAS: CASAS EL Civics Objectives; FL: Florida Civics, Family, and Community Resources Standards;
IL: Illinois Community College Board's EL/Civics Competencies

WORKSHEET	CIVICS OBJECTIVES / COMPETENCIES (CASAS/FL/IL)
15	**CASAS** (21) Recognize the importance of good parenting skills that help children at different levels of development, and access resources available in the community to help parents.
16	**CASAS** (22) Access leisure-time, cultural, and/or recreational resources.
17	**CASAS** (23) Access and use community service and government agency information.
18	**CASAS** (24) Identify and access community and government resources in order to prevent accidents, avoid becoming a crime victim, report accidents or crimes, and request assistance in case of an accident or crime.
19	**CASAS** (26) Identify and access free or low-cost medical, dental, and other health-care services.
	IL HE1. Check the eligibility requirements for public health services.
	FL Collect and share information with other students on health-related agencies in the community.
20	**CASAS** (27) Demonstrate knowledge of health and safety precautions by participating in activities such as CPR and first aid training.
	IL CR4. Identify safety education programs available in their community for adults and children.
21	**CASAS** (28) Access the health-care system and be able to interact with the providers.
22	**CASAS** (30) Demonstrate how to use pharmacies/drug stores and medicines.
23	**CASAS** (46) Access resources for nutrition education and information related to the purchase and preparation of healthy foods.
24	**CASAS** (33) Identify and access employment and training resources needed to obtain and keep a job.
25	**CASAS** (36) Identify work-related safety regulations, standards, and procedures.
26	**CASAS** (37) Identify and demonstrate qualities of an effective employee in the American workplace in order to get a job, keep a job, or get a better job.
27	**CASAS** (40) Respond to questions about the history and government of the United States in order to be successful in the naturalization process.
28	**CASAS** (43) Identify environmental problems, access local environmental organizations and government agencies, and recognize appropriate steps for resolution of the problems.
29	**CASAS** (44) Identify, access, and complete applications to agencies that provide identification cards and/or other services such as the DMV.
30	**CASAS** (1) Identify, evaluate, and compare financial service options in the community such as banks, credit unions, check-cashing services, and credit cards.
31	**IL** HO1. Identify types of housing in the community.
32	**IL** HO2. Locate agencies to assist with finding housing. / HO7. Identify resources for home ownership information.
33	**CASAS** (46) Access resources for nutrition education and information related to the purchase and preparation of healthy foods.
34	**CASAS** (14) Identify educational opportunities and research education / training required to achieve a personal goal.
35	**CASAS** (9) Locate and analyze preschool and childcare services in the community, and identify procedures for enrolling a child and participating in a preschool or childcare program.

WORKSHEET	CIVICS OBJECTIVES / COMPETENCIES (CASAS/FL/IL)
36	**IL** SC7. Identify special services available to students in local school districts. / SC9. Identify eligibility requirements for special school programs, such as Head Start, free lunch, enrichment, and tutoring.
37	**CASAS** (15) Demonstrate basic knowledge and awareness of the emergency services available in the community and ways to contact and use emergency services and legal assistance agencies.
	IL CR5. Prepare a list of emergency telephone numbers for their communities.
38	**CASAS** (20) Access and evaluate extracurricular community activities for children and adults.
39	**CASAS** (23) Access and use community service and government agency information.
40	**CASAS** (25) Identify and describe volunteer opportunities in the community.
	FL Provide evidence of participation as an active volunteer in a community service program. / Provide evidence of volunteering at your child's school.
41	**IL** SC1. Identify how schools are organized in the U.S. school system. / SC2. Identify the organization of grades with schools within their local school districts. / SC3. Identify the ages of children that public schools are required to serve. / SC5. Explain the organization of their local school districts and school boards.
42	**CASAS** (23) Access and use community service and government agency information.
43	**FL** Prepare a schedule for reading with child/children at home. / Develop a written plan for checking child's/children's backpack regularly.
44	**CASAS** (23) Access and use community service and government agency information.
	IL CR7. Locate a public library in their community and apply for a library card.
45	**FL** Prepare a sample note to a teacher about a child. / Prepare a sample note to a teacher requesting a parent-teacher conference.
46	**FL** Identify and map the emergency shelters located in the community, and share this information with other students.
47	**CASAS** (10) Identify, locate, and map important places in the community, the state, and the country, and list services available and/or importance of each location.
48	**IL** HE1. Check eligibility requirements for public health services. / HE3. Explain the difference between public and private health care.
49	**IL** HE4. Locate public and private health-care providers in their communities. / HE5. Identify community resources for wellness programs including prenatal care, immunizations, and screenings.
50	**CASAS** (32) Locate, analyze, and describe job requirements, licenses, credentials, etc., needed for specific jobs, and identify resources available to help access the information.
51	**CASAS** (33) Identify and access employment and training resources needed to obtain and keep a job.
52	**CASAS** (35) Identify procedures for protecting employment rights and access resources that support and assist the worker.
53	**CASAS** (33) Identify and access employment and training resources needed to obtain and keep a job.
54	**CASAS** (19) Identify the rights of immigrants in the United States, and access local and state agencies that specialize in these rights.
55	**CASAS** (38) Identify the basic organization and access to local, county, state, and/or federal government.

WORKSHEET	CIVICS OBJECTIVES / COMPETENCIES (CASAS/FL/IL)
56	**IL** CR8. Contact local government officials to voice their opinions. / DP6. Identify ways to contact their elected officials. / DP7. Contact an elected official to express their opinions.
57	**CASAS** (44) Identify, access, and complete applications to agencies that provide identification cards and/or other services such as the DMV.
58	**CASAS** (42) Identify people and events in local, state, and federal history.
59	**CASAS** (39) Identify and discuss the voting process, including rights and responsibilities, and the political process in the United States.
	IL DP1. Define voting. / DP2. Explain the importance of voting. / DP3. List the requirements for voting in the United States.
60	**CASAS** (10) Identify, locate, and map important places in the community, the state, and the country, and list services available and/or importance of each location.
61	**CASAS** (2) Access community or commercial agencies to resolve a consumer complaint.
62	**CASAS** (3) Develop a business plan for a small business in order to participate in the economic growth of the community.
63	**CASAS** (5) Interpret lease and rental agreements and recognize responsibilities of renters and landlords.
64	**CASAS** (2) Access community or commercial agencies to resolve a consumer complaint.
65	**CASAS** (5) Interpret lease and rental agreements and recognize responsibilities of renters and landlords.
66	**CASAS** (1) Identify, evaluate, and compare financial service options in the community such as banks, credit unions, check-cashing services, and credit cards.
67	**CASAS** (10) Identify, locate, and map important places in the community, the state, and the country, and list services and/or importance of each location.
68	**CASAS** (7) Identify effective ways to safeguard families and homes, including the use of community and governmental resources.
69	**IL** SC4. Describe the similarities and differences between the U.S. school system and the school system in their native countries. / SC8. Differentiate between public and private schools.
70	**CASAS** (29) Interpret medical insurance coverage, and resolve insurance coverage problems and issues with medical service providers.
71	**CASAS** (31) Identify, describe, and access available resources in the community for prevention and treatment of substance abuse.
72	**CASAS** (33) Identify and access employment and training resources needed to obtain and keep a job.
73	**CASAS** (33) Identify and access employment and training resources needed to obtain and keep a job.
74	**CASAS** (38) Identify the basic organization and access to local, county, state, and/or federal government.
	FL-citizenship 05.08 Explain government election procedure at the local, state, and national level.
75	**CASAS** (39) Identify and discuss the voting process, including rights and responsibilities, and the political process in the United States.
	FL Provide evidence of obtaining a voter's registration card.

WORKSHEET	CIVICS OBJECTIVES / COMPETENCIES (CASAS/FL/IL)
76	**CASAS** (44) Identify, access, and complete applications to agencies that provide identification cards and/or other services such as the DMV.
77	**CASAS** (45) Identify basic features of the local, state, and federal legal system including individual rights, laws, and ordinances as well as procedures for obtaining legal help.
78	**CASAS** (19) Identify the rights of immigrants in the United States, and access local and state agencies that specialize in these rights.
	FL-citizenship 05.09 Identify who has the right to vote.
79	**CASAS** (19) Identify the rights of immigrants in the United States, and access local and state agencies that specialize in these rights.
	IL DP9. Explain rights to legal assistance.
80	**CASAS** (38) Identify the basic organization and access to local, county, state, and/or federal government.
	FL-citizenship 05.05 Identify the structure and function of government at the local and state levels. / 05.06 Identify types of local government.
81	**FL-citizenship** 03.01 Identify White House as official home for U.S. president. / 03.02 Recognize the U.S. Capitol as a meeting place for the U.S. Congress.
82	**FL-citizenship** 05.01 Explain the concept of the U.S. Constitution. / 05.03 Explain the importance of the Bill of Rights.
83	**CASAS** (40) Respond to questions about the history and government of the United States in order to be successful in the naturalization process.
	FL-citizenship 04.08 Recognize the importance of the American Revolution.
84	**CASAS** (42) Identify people and events in local, state, and federal history.
	FL-citizenship 04.03 Identify George Washington and explain his contribution.
85	**FL-citizenship** 04.04 Identify Patrick Henry and explain his contribution.
86	**CASAS** (42) Identify people and events in local, state, and federal history.
	FL-citizenship 04.02 Identify Thomas Jefferson and explain his contribution.
87	**CASAS** (40) Respond to questions about the history and government of the United States in order to be successful in the naturalization process
	FL-citizenship 03.04 Demonstrate knowledge of significance of U.S. flag. / 04.01 Identify Francis Scott Key and explain his contribution.
88	**CASAS** (40) Respond to questions about the history and government of the United States in order to be successful in the naturalization process.
	FL-citizenship 04.09 Explain the causes of the American Civil War.
89	**CASAS** (40) Respond to questions about the history and government of the United States in order to be successful in the naturalization process.
	FL-citizenship 04.05 Demonstrate knowledge of the significance and consequences of the Civil Rights Movement. / 04.06 Identify civil rights leaders.
90	**FL-citizenship** 03.0 Identify U.S. symbols. / 03.03 Recognize the Liberty Bell as the image of freedom for the United States. / 03.05 Know significance of Statue of Liberty.

Worksheet 1 *It's in the bank.*

A Label the pictures.

| an ATM card   cash   a check   a credit card |

1. _____cash_____   2. _____   3. _____   4. _____

B Read about bank accounts. Match the words with the definitions.

> There are two kinds of accounts for money at the bank: <u>savings accounts</u> and <u>checking accounts</u>. You can <u>deposit</u> money into a savings account and earn extra money for using the bank. This is called <u>interest</u>. Checking accounts do not usually earn interest. You can write a <u>check</u> or use a <u>debit card</u> when you want to buy something. You do not have to carry <u>cash</u> with you.

1. savings account __d__
2. checking account ____
3. deposit ____
4. interest ____
5. check or debit card ____
6. cash ____

a. an account that does not usually earn interest
b. put money in the bank
c. use when you do not want to pay with cash
d. an account with interest
e. dollar bills or coins
f. extra money you earn with a savings account

C Number the sentences in the correct order.

How to use an ATM card to withdraw (take out) money

__3__ Select "Withdrawal" to take money from your checking account.

____ Take the money out of the machine.

__1__ Put your ATM card in the ATM machine.

____ Enter your personal identification number (PIN).

____ Take your ATM card and receipt.

____ Enter the amount of money you want.

© Cambridge University Press 2010   Photocopiable

Worksheet 2 *Finding a place to live*

A Look at the chart. Match the housing abbreviations with the definitions.

Housing abbreviations	Definitions
BA	bathroom
BR	bedroom
inc.	included
nr.	near
W/D	washer and dryer

1. inc. _d_   a. bedroom
2. BA ____   b. washer and dryer
3. W/D ____   c. near
4. BR ____   d. included
5. nr. ____   e. bathroom

B Look at the housing advertisements. Answer the questions.

FOR RENT		
Sunny Gardens	**University Place**	**North Park**
Apt.	Apt.	House
2BR / 1BA	2BR / 2BA	3BR / 2BA
Quiet	Nr. trains	Nr. buses
Some utilities inc.	All utilities inc.	W/D
$800 / month	$1,000 / month	$1,250 / month

1. Which place is near trains? _____ *University Place* _____

2. Which place is near buses? _____

3. Which place has some utilities included? _____

4. Which place has a washer and dryer? _____

5. Which place has one bathroom? _____

C Look at the ads in Exercise B. Circle *T* (true) or *F* (false). Correct the false sentences.

1. University Place has ~~some~~ utilities included.   T   Ⓕ
                     all

2. Sunny Gardens costs $800 each month.   T   F

3. North Park costs $1,200 each month.   T   F

4. University Place has three bathrooms.   T   F

5. North Park has three bedrooms.   T   F

© Cambridge University Press 2010   **Photocopiable**

Consumer economics

Worksheet 3 *Housing issues*

A Match the correct word with each picture.

leaking	jammed	broken

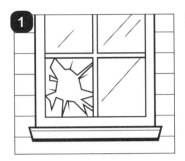 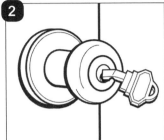 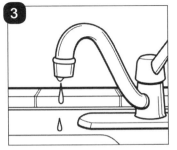

1. The window is _____ .

2. The lock is _____ .

3. The faucet is _____ .

B Read the conversation. Complete the chart.

Sarah Hi, Sam. What's wrong?

Sam I have a problem. The faucet is leaking and the toilet is broken.

Sarah You should call a plumber.

Sam The electricity isn't working and the lightbulb won't turn on, either.

Sarah You need to call an electrician. Any other problems?

Sam Yes. My window is also broken.

Sarah You should call your landlord about it.

Sam Thanks. I'll do that.

Problems	Solutions
The faucet is leaking.	Call a plumber.

C Talk with a partner. Ask and answer the questions.

1. Who do you contact for housing problems?

2. What do you do if your electricity isn't working?

© Cambridge University Press 2010   Photocopiable

Worksheet 4 *Keeping safe*

A Read the conversation with a partner. Answer the questions.

Operator 911. What's the emergency?
Cynthia Someone broke into our house!
Operator What's the address?
Cynthia 678 Maple Drive.
Operator What's your name?
Cynthia Cynthia Jones.
Operator The police will be there in a few minutes. Stay calm.
Cynthia Thank you.

1. Who did Cynthia call? _____

2. What is the emergency? _____

3. What is the address of the house? _____

4. Who is coming to the house? _____

B Match the correct sentence with each picture.

Lock your doors.	Join a Neighborhood Watch Association.	Call 911 in an emergency situation.

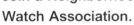   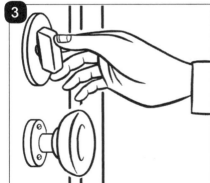

1. _____

2. _____

3. _____

C Talk with a partner. Ask and answer the questions.

1. Are you a part of a Neighborhood Watch Program? _____

2. What are other ways you can stay safe in your neighborhood?

_____

© Cambridge University Press 2010 **Photocopiable**

Worksheet 5 | *Community cleanup*

A Read about a community problem. Number the steps in the correct order.

Before   After

A few years ago, my neighborhood was not very nice. We did not have a park where our children could play. There was an empty lot near the houses. It was dirty. There was no playground. It was not safe for our children.

We talked about the problem in our Neighborhood Association meeting. We decided to clean up the empty lot. Some people cleaned up the trash. Other people planted a tree. A store donated playground equipment. Now we have a nice little park. Our children like to play there after school and on the weekends.

_____ People in the Neighborhood Association planted a tree.

_____ A local store donated playground equipment to the community.

_____ Now we have a nice park in our neighborhood.

_1_ Our neighborhood had an empty lot. It was dirty.

_____ The Neighborhood Association decided to clean the lot.

_____ We had a Neighborhood Association meeting.

B Talk with a partner. Ask and answer the questions.

1. What are some problems in your community? _____

_____

2. What can you do to help solve the problems? _____

_____

© Cambridge University Press 2010   Photocopiable

Worksheet 6 Important places in the community

A Look at the map. Complete the list.

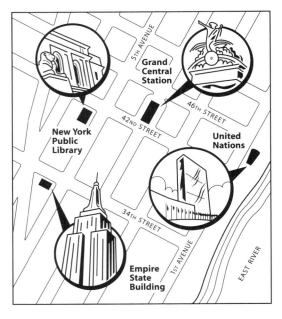

Important places in New York City
1. *Grand Central Station*
2.
3.
4.

B Look at the sign. Answer the questions.

Welcome to the Empire State Building!

Address: 350 5th Ave.
New York, NY 10018

Admission prices:
Toddlers (5 or younger) .... Free
Child (6–11) $12.92
Youth (12–17) $16.61
Adults (18–61) $18.45
Seniors (62+) $16.61

Hours: Open 365 days a year
8:00 a.m. to 2:00 a.m.
7 days a week

1. What is the address of the Empire State Building?

   _____

2. What is the admission price for a 12-year-old?

   _____

3. What time does the Empire State Building open?

   _____

4. How many days is it open during the year?

   _____

C Work with a partner.

1. Draw a map of your neighborhood or city on a separate piece of paper. Include important places on the map.

2. What is one important place in your city? Find out the following information:

   a. address: _____

   b. admission prices: _____

   c. hours: _____

Photocopiable © Cambridge University Press 2010

Worksheet 7 — *We come from different places.*

A Look at the picture. Read the story. Complete the chart.

There are many students at Mason Community College. They are from different countries and different cultures. Lorena is from Mexico. She speaks Spanish. Kalifa is from Somalia. She speaks Somali. Fabio is from Brazil. He speaks Portuguese. Shen is from China. He speaks Mandarin. Yuri is from Russia. He speaks Russian. Diane is from the United States. She speaks English.

Name of student	Country	Language
Lorena	Mexico	Spanish

B Interview your classmates. Complete the chart.

What's your name?	Where are you from?	What language do you speak?
1.		
2.		
3.		

© Cambridge University Press 2010   Photocopiable

Worksheet 8 *Jennifer gets a driver's license.*

A Match.

1

a. You can only turn left in this lane.

2

b. You have to look out for pedestrians (people crossing the street).

3

c. Slow down here and watch for traffic, and then continue driving.

B Read about Jennifer. Circle the correct answers.

> Jennifer wanted a driver's license. She looked online to find the address of the Department of Motor Vehicles (DMV). She studied for the California driver's exam. She used a driver's manual. She studied traffic and road rules. She also practiced driving. She practiced turning, driving in reverse, and parking.
>
> When Jennifer got to the DMV, she took the written test and the driving test. She also had a vision exam. Jennifer passed all of her tests. Now she has a driver's license! She is very happy.

1. Where did Jennifer find the address for the Department of Motor Vehicles?
   a. She found it in the phone book.
   b. She found it online.

2. What did Jennifer study before the test?
   a. She studied about traffic and road rules.
   b. She studied about cars.

3. What did Jennifer practice?
   a. She practiced for the written test.
   b. She practiced turning and parking.

4. Did Jennifer pass all of her tests?
   a. Yes, she did.
   b. No, she didn't.

C Talk with a partner. Ask and answer the questions.

1. What are some other traffic signs?
2. What are other services offered at the DMV?

© Cambridge University Press 2010 **Photocopiable**

Worksheet 9 *School matters*

A Read the story. Complete the school registration form.

> Juana Martinez is registering her son for school. Her son's name is Miguel Martinez. His date of birth is March 8, 2003. He was born in Mexico. Juana's address is 1234 Spring Street, Denver, Colorado. Her zip code is 80220. Juana's phone number is (303) 555-6789. The last school that Miguel attended was The Sandbox Preschool. Juana's brother is the emergency contact. His name is Javier Delgado. His phone number is (303) 555-8876.

Brown Elementary School Registration Form

Name of student ___*Martinez*_____
 1 (Last name)   2 (First name)

Date of Birth _____ / _____ / _____ **Country of birth** _____
 3 (Month)   (Day)   (Year)   4

Sex Male _____ Female _____
 5

Address _____ **Zip code** _____
 6   7

Phone number _____
 8

Last school attended _____
 9

Emergency contact _____ _____
 10 (name)   11 (phone number)

B Complete the conversation. Then practice with a partner.

| date of birth   name   phone number   school |

Secretary Brown Elementary _____ .
 1
How may I help you?

Juana My son is sick today. He can't come to school.

Secretary What's your son's _____ ?
 2

Juana Miguel Martinez.

Secretary What is his _____ ?
 3

Juana March 8, 2003.

Secretary And what is your _____ ?
 4

Juana It's (303) 555-6789.

Secretary What's the matter with Miguel?

Juana He has the flu.

Secretary Thank you. I hope he feels better soon.

© Cambridge University Press 2010   Photocopiable

Worksheet 10 | *In the case of an emergency*

A Look at the picture. What happened? Talk with a partner.

B Number the sentences in the correct order.

_____ She called 911.

_1_ Carol was at home.

_____ She fell off a ladder.

_____ Her head hurt a lot.

_____ She hit her head on the ground.

C Read the conversation with a partner. Answer the questions.

Operator 911. What's the emergency?

Carol I fell off a ladder and hurt my head. It hurts a lot.

Operator Where are you?

Carol I'm at home.

Operator Is anyone at home with you?

Carol No.

Operator What's your name and address?

Carol My name is Carol Jackson. I live at 8 Lake Road in Evanston.

Operator An ambulance is coming to your home in ten minutes. The ambulance is going to take you to the hospital.

Carol Thank you.

1. What happened to Carol? *Carol fell off a ladder.* _____

2. What hurts? _____

3. Where is Carol? _____

4. What is an ambulance? _____

D Talk with a partner. Ask and answer the questions.

1. What should you do in an emergency?

2. Did you ever call 911?

© Cambridge University Press 2010 **Photocopiable**

Worksheet 11 *Emergency or nonemergency?*

A Read the paragraph. Answer the questions.

> ## Emergency and Nonemergency Situations
>
> What is an emergency? An emergency requires immediate action. If you don't do something immediately, there could be a bad result. For example, if there is a fire, you should call the fire department. If you see a crime taking place, you should call the police department. If your child accidentally drinks something poisonous, like a cleaning product, you should call poison control.
>
> A nonemergency is not as serious. For example, if you burn your finger, you can put your hand in cold water. You don't have to call the fire department. If you hurt your back, you can call a doctor. You don't have to call 911.

1. What is an emergency situation? _____

2. What is a nonemergency situation? _____

B Match the correct sentence with each picture.

| Call 911 about a fire. | Put your hand in cold water. | Call 911 about an accident. |

1. _____

2. _____

3. _____

C Read the sentences. Circle *emergency* or *nonemergency*.

1. The chef burned his hand.   emergency   nonemergency

2. There is a car accident.   emergency   nonemergency

3. A house is on fire.   emergency   nonemergency

D Talk with a partner. Name two emergency and two nonemergency situations.

© Cambridge University Press 2010   Photocopiable

Worksheet 12 *Agencies that can help you*

A Read the conversation. Answer the questions.

Sarah Hi, Maria. You look sad.

Maria I'm having some problems at home.

Sarah What's the matter?

Maria Well, my husband gets very angry sometimes. He hits me. I don't know what to do.

Sarah Maria, that's called domestic violence. Domestic violence is violence that happens between family members. There are agencies that can help you.

Maria How can I get help?

Sarah You can look in the telephone book or use the Internet. There are domestic violence hotlines you can call for help.

Maria What are "hotlines"?

Sarah Hotlines are phone numbers you call for help with problems. People answer the phone and give you advice. You can also talk to a counselor about your problems.

Maria Thanks, Sarah. I'll look it up in the telephone book. You're a good friend.

1. What is Maria's problem? _____

2. What is domestic violence? _____

3. What does Sarah tell Maria to do? _____

4. What are hotlines? _____

5. Where can Maria find the numbers for the hotlines? _____

B Look at the page from the phone book. Work with a partner. Answer the questions.

COMMUNITY SERVICES

Crime Hotline
555-1234

Domestic Violence Hotline
555-4545

Center for Women and Children
555-6789

Community Information
555-9876

Substance Abuse Support Center
555-3421

1. What number do you call for help with crime in the community? _____

2. What number do you call for help with domestic violence? _____

3. What number do you call for help with substance abuse? _____

4. What number do you call for community information? _____

5. What number do you call for help with your child?

_____

© Cambridge University Press 2010 Photocopiable

Worksheet **13** *Community resources for senior citizens*

A Read the article. Circle the answers.

> Senior citizens sometimes need help with meals, housing, and health care. Some community and government services help senior citizens. For example, Meals on Wheels brings low-cost meals to people who are 60 and older who cannot leave their homes because of health problems. Another program is Medicare. It is the largest health insurance program in the United States. It is a government program that helps people 65 years and older with medical bills. Some seniors can pay lower rates on utility bills. Also, local senior centers have volunteers to help seniors. They help seniors with transportation, shopping, or gardening.

1. What is Meals on Wheels?
   a. It helps seniors with their medical expenses.
   b. It brings meals to seniors.
2. What is Medicare?
   a. a volunteer service for seniors
   b. a program that helps seniors with their medical expenses

3. What is a service for senior citizens?
   a. childcare services
   b. reduced rates on utility bills
4. What is a senior center?
   a. a place where volunteers help seniors
   b. It provides reduced utility bills.

B Complete the puzzle.

DOWN
1. _____ help seniors at senior centers.
4. _____ citizens are older people.

ACROSS
2. _____ on Wheels is a program that brings food to seniors.
3. Seniors can receive reduced rates on their _____ bills.
5. _____ is the United States' largest health insurance program.

© Cambridge University Press 2010   **Photocopiable**

Worksheet 14 | *Rights and responsibilities*

A Read about the rights and responsibilities of immigrants and naturalized citizens. Write *T* (true) or *F* (false). Correct the false sentences.

> Immigrants who are permanent residents in the United States have certain rights and responsibilities. They have the right to live permanently in the United States if they do not commit any crimes. They can work in the United States. They can travel outside of the United States with the correct documents. They are also protected by federal and state laws.
>
> Permanent residents also have certain responsibilities. They have to obey, or follow, all the laws of the United States and the state where they live. They have to pay income taxes. Men, ages 18 through 26, have to register with the Selective Service.
>
> Many permanent residents of the United States want to become naturalized U.S. citizens. Naturalized U.S. citizens have the same rights as U.S.-born citizens except that they cannot become the president of the United States.

__*F*__ Permanent residents ~~cannot~~ *can* work in the United States.

_____ Permanent residents don't have to pay income taxes.

_____ Men, ages 18–25, have to register with the Selective Service.

_____ Permanent residents cannot become the president of the United States.

B Complete the story.

citizen	responsibilities	Selective Service	taxes

> Jean is from Mali. He is a permanent resident of the United States. He has certain
>
> rights and _____ . He can apply for a job. He is protected
>   1
>
> by the laws. He has to obey all the laws, too. He has to pay federal and state income
>
> _____ . He is 24 years old. He must register with the
>   2
>
> _____ . He can travel back to Mali or to other countries.
>   3
>
> Jean's goal is to become a naturalized _____ of the
>   4
>
> United States in four years.

C Look in a phone book or use the Internet. Answer the questions.

1. What is a local agency that provides immigrant services? _____

2. What services does it offer? _____

3. What is the address? What hours is it open? _____

© Cambridge University Press 2010   **Photocopiable**

Worksheet 15 *What makes a good parent?*

A Look at the Web site about good parenting. Match the word with the definition.

5 Parenting Tips

1. Love and support your child.
2. Correct your child when he/she does something wrong. Explain to your child what he/she did wrong and explain the consequences (results).
3. Look for family literacy classes in your area. These classes teach you to help your child with his/her homework.
4. Keep your child safe in your car. Always use a car seat for babies and younger children. Use seat belts, too. These can save your child's life!
5. If you have time, volunteer at your child's school. Talk to the teacher about your child's progress. Talk to your child about what he/she is learning at school.

1. support	a. teach parents to help their children with their homework
2. consequences	b. keeps your child safe in the car
3. family literacy classes	c. to encourage; to help your child feel confident
4. car seat	d. how well your child is doing at school
5. progress	e. results

B Complete the paragraph.

family literacy classes   progress   consequences

   Belinda tries to be a good parent. Her son, Romero, sometimes doesn't

want to turn off the TV and do his homework. She explains to him the

_____ of not doing his homework. She also
                1

takes _____ so she can help him with
                2

difficult homework assignments. Sometimes, she volunteers at his school.

Every two months, she meets with his teacher. They talk about Romero's

_____ at school.
         3

C Talk with a partner. Ask and answer the questions.

1. What do you think is the most important parenting tip in Exercise A? Why?
2. What do you think is the best way to help a child at school?

© Cambridge University Press 2010   Photocopiable

Worksheet 16 *What should we do this weekend?*

A Look at the poster. Answer the questions.

> *The Arts Society Presents*
> # Romeo and Juliet
> **ADMISSION IS FREE!**
> June 12–16
> 7 p.m.
> Jacobs Park
> Tucson, Arizona
>
> Bring a blanket or a chair and a picnic dinner, and enjoy an evening under the stars!
>
> **For more information, call 555-6432**

1. What is the name of the play? *Romeo and Juliet* _____

2. How much is admission? _____

3. What time can you see the play? _____

4. Where is the play? _____

5. What should you bring to the play? _____

6. What number can you call for more information? _____

B Talk with a partner. Read the conversation. Complete the chart.

Mike Hi, Nancy. What are you doing this weekend?

Nancy I'm not sure. There's a free family arts festival this Saturday. My kids love the art projects and puppet shows.

Mike That sounds great! Why don't you go?

Nancy Well, there's a film festival on the same day. I'd like to go to that, too. It only costs $5 to see a lot of different movies.

Mike That also sounds like fun. Well, I'm taking my kids to the art museum. There's free admission on Sunday.

Nancy There's so much going on this weekend. I can't decide!

Activity	Day	Admission
family arts festival	Saturday	free

© Cambridge University Press 2010   Photocopiable

Worksheet 17 Finding local community and government services

A Look at the telephone directory page. Write the correct telephone numbers. Discuss your answers with a partner.

GOVERNMENT	
Fire Dept.	555-3589
Recycling and Waste Dept.	555-7878
Library Services Dept.	555-9873
Parks and Recreation Dept.	555-3412
Police Dept.	555-5432
Transportation and Traffic Safety Dept.	555-3321
Water Dept.	555-0863

1. You saw someone steal your neighbor's bicycle. *555-5432*

2. You want to recycle your bottles and cans. _____

3. The traffic light on your street is broken. _____

4. The water stopped running in your house. _____

5. You are looking for a place to take your children to play outside. _____

6. You want to get a library card. _____

7. You need a smoke detector in your apartment. _____

B Look at the list of community services. Answer the questions. Discuss your answers with a partner.

> Employment and Career Services
> Hospitals
> Medical and Dental Services
> Library Services
> Parenting Services
> Senior Services
> Volunteer Opportunities

1. Which of these community services do you use? Why?

   _____

   _____

2. Which of these community services do you not use? Why not?

   _____

   _____

© Cambridge University Press 2010   Photocopiable

Worksheet **18** *Crime or suspicious activity?*

A Read the article. Complete John's crime report.

John Smith saw a crime yesterday. His neighbor's window was broken. Then he saw a strange man leave the house and get into a car. The man was about 5 feet 8 inches tall and weighed about 150 pounds. He had long brown hair, and he had a tattoo. The car was an old red pickup truck. John wrote down the license number. It was AGD789. John talked to his neighbor later. His neighbor's house was robbed. John filled out a crime report at the police station.

CRIME REPORT

Last Name _____Smith_____   **First Name** _____John_____
                    1   2

Do you know who is responsible? (circle one)   Yes   No
                                                        3

Physical description _____
                                              4

Height ____   **Weight** ____   **Hair color** ____
          5   6   7

Vehicle involved

Type _____   **Color** _____   **License No.** _____
        8   9   10

What happened?

_____

_____

_____
                        11

B Work with a partner. Complete the chart.

	Crime	Suspicious Activity (possible crime)
1. Two men rob a bank.	☐	☐
2. A person looks into someone's window.	☐	☐
3. A car runs into another car and leaves.	☐	☐
4. Someone is looking in car windows in a parking lot.	☐	☐
5. A car drives down up and down a street many times.	☐	☐
6. A person breaks into your neighbor's house.	☐	☐

© Cambridge University Press 2010   Photocopiable

Worksheet 19 *Where can Lucia find low-cost health-care services?*

A Read the conversation with a partner. Match the words with the definitions.

Philippe Lucia, what's the matter?

Lucia My son needs to go to the doctor, but I don't have a lot of money.

Philippe Do you have health insurance?

Lucia I don't think so. What is it?

Philippe Health insurance pays for your visits to the doctor, the hospital, and for prescriptions. Some people get it from their employers or pay for it themselves.

Lucia No, I don't think I get that at work. What should I do?

Philippe You could go to a public health center. They give you health care even if you don't have health insurance. You only pay what you can afford. That means you pay as much as you can.

Lucia And they will help my son?

Philippe The center will tell you if your son is eligible, if he can be treated there. It depends on how much money you earn and how many people live in your house.

Lucia How can I find a public health center?

Philippe Use the Internet and search for "find a health center." Type in your address, city, and zip code. You'll get a list of health centers near you.

Lucia Thanks.

1. health insurance
2. public health center
3. eligible
4. afford

a. a place where you can receive medical care without health insurance
b. as much as you can pay
c. It pays for the doctor, the hospital, and for prescriptions.
d. able to be treated

B Look at the Web site. Answer the questions.

> **Health Resources and Services**
> **FIND A HEALTH CENTER NEAR YOU!**
> No health insurance?
> You can go to a public health center near you.
> You pay what you can afford. Health centers provide:
> • checkups when you are well, help when you are sick
> • pregnancy care, immunizations, and checkups for your children
> • dental care and prescription drugs for your family
> • mental health and substance abuse care (help for addictions)

1. How much do you pay at a public health center? _____

2. Can your children get checkups at a public health center? _____

3. Can you get dental care at a public health center? _____

4. Can you get help for addictions at a public health center? _____

© Cambridge University Press 2010   Photocopiable

Worksheet 20 | *Health and safety precautions*

A Match the correct sentence with each picture.

a) The house is on fire.   b) There is no fence around the pool.   c) She burned her fingers.

1. _____

2. _____

3. _____

B A *precaution* is something you do to stop something bad or dangerous from happening. Match the problem with the safety precaution.

Problem

1. The house is on fire.
2. She burned her fingers.
3. The toddler is going into the pool alone.

Safety precaution

a. Put a fence around the pool. Watch your children at all times.

b. Turn off all electrical appliances before you leave the house. Keep a fire extinguisher in the house.

c. Don't touch a hot pan with your fingers. Use a potholder or oven glove (these are used for holding hot pots and pans).

C Read the first aid tips. Circle *T* for true or *F* for false. Correct the false sentences.

FIRST AID: What to do if you have a burn

- First, make sure the burn is not too serious. If the burn is very large or painful, go to the hospital or call your doctor.
- For minor or small burns, hold the burn under cold running water for 5 minutes. Don't use ice.
- Then, cover the burn with a gauze (light cloth) bandage. Look for the word *sterile* on the gauze package. *Sterile* means it's clean and free from bacteria (something that causes infections). Don't use fluffy cotton or any ointments.

1. If the burn is very large, go to the hospital.   T   F
2. For small burns, use ice.   T   F
3. Cover the burn with fluffy cotton.   T   F

© Cambridge University Press 2010   Photocopiable

Worksheet 21 *I have a terrible headache!*

A Read the conversation. Circle the answers.

Dr. Brown Good morning. How are you?

Jim Not so good. I have a terrible headache, and my body aches.

Dr. Brown How long have you had these symptoms?

Jim For two days. I also have a fever. I feel hot and cold all the time.

Dr. Brown You have the flu. Take these pills every 4 hours until your temperature goes down. Also, drink plenty of liquids and get rest.

Jim Thank you. I'll do that.

1. What are Jim's symptoms?
   a. He is thirsty all the time, and he can't sleep.
   b. He has a headache, and his body aches.

2. What's the matter with Jim?
   a. He has the flu.
   b. He has a broken leg.

3. What does the doctor prescribe?
   a. Take pills every 4 hours.
   b. Take pills every 6 hours.

4. What else does the doctor tell him to do?
   a. He needs to go to the hospital.
   b. He needs to drink plenty of liquids and get rest.

B Look at the Web site. Answer the questions.

Local business results for health clinics in Tucson, AZ:	
Marana Health Clinic	555-8909
Freedom Health Center	555-0984
El Rio Health Center	555-8989
Center for Women and Children	555-6543
HIV Testing Clinic	555-1234

1. What's the phone number for the Marana Health Clinic? _____

2. What health clinic has the phone number 555-0984? _____

3. What's the phone number for the Center for Women and Children? _____

4. What's the phone number for the HIV Testing Clinic? _____

© Cambridge University Press 2010   Photocopiable

Worksheet 22 *Looking at medicine labels*

A Look at the medicine label. Circle the answers.

Drug facts
Active ingredient (in each tablet) **Purpose**   Ibuprofen 200mg .... Pain reliever
Uses Temporary relief of headaches, toothaches, colds, and backaches.
Warning   Do not use if you have allergies to pain relievers.
Directions   Adults and children 12 years and over: Take 1 tablet every 4 to 6 hours.   Do not take more than 6 tablets in 24 hours.   Do not give to children under 12.   Do not take more than directed.

1. What is this medicine for?
   a. headaches
   b. burns

2. How many tablets should you take if you have allergies to pain relievers?
   a. two tablets
   b. no tablets

3. How many tablets should adults take?
   a. two tablets
   b. one tablet

4. How many tablets should children under 12 take?
   a. no tablets
   b. one tablet

B Read the phone conversation with a partner. Answer the questions.

Pharmacist Miller's Drugs. How can I help you?

Sherry I bought cold medicine from your pharmacy today. I have a question.

Pharmacist All right.

Sherry I have a very bad cold. Can I take three tablets every two hours?

Pharmacist No, you have to follow the instructions on the label. Take two tablets every 4 hours.

Sherry OK. Thank you very much.

1. What's the matter with Sherry? _____

2. What kind of medicine did she buy today? _____

3. Where are the instructions for the medicine? _____

4. What does the pharmacist say? _____

© Cambridge University Press 2010 Photocopiable

Worksheet 23 *Eating healthy!*

A Read the conversation. Answer the questions.

Rachel Hi, Ahmed. How are you doing?

Ahmed I don't feel good. I'm always tired. I have to work long hours, and I don't have time to make good, healthy meals.

Rachel What kind of food do you eat?

Ahmed Fast food. I go to restaurants after work.

Rachel You should think about changing the way you eat.

Ahmed What do you mean?

Rachel Well, the U.S. Department of Agriculture says we should eat a lot of grains, vegetables, fruits, and milk products. We shouldn't eat a lot of oils, fried foods, and meats.

Ahmed I eat a lot of hamburgers and hot dogs.

Rachel Why don't you try eating more salads and pasta? You can try it for a week and see how you feel.

Ahmed I'll do that. Thanks for your help.

1. What kind of food does Ahmed eat? _____

2. What does Rachel suggest? _____

3. What does the U.S. Department of Agriculture (USDA) say? _____

_____

B Label the picture. Use *fruit*, *grain*, *milk*, and *vegetable*.

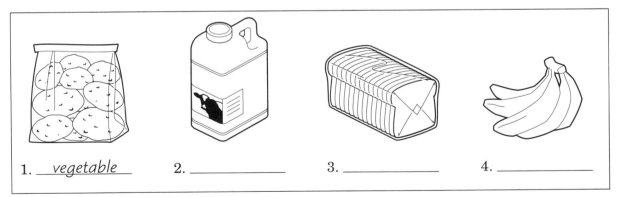

1. _*vegetable*_   2. _____   3. _____   4. _____

C Work with a partner. List examples in the chart below.

fruits	grains	meat	milk (dairy)	oils	vegetables
apples					

© Cambridge University Press 2010   Photocopiable

Worksheet 24 — *Which job do you prefer?*

A Match the abbreviations with the definitions.

1. Mon. – Fri. _d_   a. part time
2. F/T ____   b. 10 dollars per hour
3. no exp. nec. ____   c. car and driver's license needed
4. car and DL needed ____   d. Monday through Friday
5. P/T ____   e. full time
6. $10/hr. ____   f. no experience necessary

B Look at the help-wanted ads. Circle the answers.

Salesperson	**Housekeeper**	**Waiter**
F/T, Mon. – Fri.	P/T afternoons	P/T evenings
$10/hr.	$9/hr.	$8/hr.
Car and DL needed	Exp. nec.	No exp. nec.
Exp. nec.	555-9876	555-3245
555-7878		

1. Which job pays $9 per hour?
   a. salesperson
   b. housekeeper
   c. waiter

2. Which job is full time?
   a. salesperson
   b. housekeeper
   c. waiter

3. Which job is for people with no experience?
   a. salesperson
   b. housekeeper
   c. waiter

4. What do you need for the salesperson job?
   a. a car
   b. a driver's license
   c. a car and a driver's license

C Talk with your classmates. Complete the chart. Use the information in Exercise B.

Which job do you prefer?		
Name	**Job**	**Why?**
Melissa	salesperson	It's full time.

© Cambridge University Press 2010   Photocopiable

Worksheet 25 *On-the-job safety*

A Match the signs with the definitions.

1.

2.

3.

4.

5.

a. No smoking!

b. Wet floor: Don't walk here.

c. Wear a hard hat in this area to protect your head.

d. Flammable: can catch fire easily

e. Biohazard: can cause harm to your health

B Read about job safety procedures. Complete the sentences.

> It is important to follow safety rules at work. Betty works at a bakery. She wears a hairnet so that her hair doesn't get into the food. Ruben works at a construction site. He wears a hard hat to protect his head. Sarah works in a laboratory. She wears safety goggles to protect her eyes.
>
> Dangerous or harmful things can happen at work every day. Read all the signs and warnings at work. They are important. Know where the fire extinguisher is in case something catches fire. A fire extinguisher can help to stop fires.

fire extinguisher	hairnet	hard hat	safety goggles	warnings

1. Betty wears a _____ *hairnet* _____ at the bakery.

2. Ruben wears a _____ at the construction site.

3. Sarah wears _____ in the laboratory.

4. Read all the signs and _____ at work.

5. Use a _____ in case of fire.

© Cambridge University Press 2010   Photocopiable

Worksheet 26 *What makes a good employee?*

A Read. Why is Juan a good worker? Make a list.

Juan is a nursing assistant at a hospital. He is very happy to have a good job. Juan works hard and follows all the rules at his job. He arrives at work on time. He does all the work that he needs to do. He is friendly and works well with the other people at the hospital. He is dependable and responsible. He always looks neat and wears a clean uniform. Juan is also studying English at night school. He is learning to communicate well with the other employees at his job.

1. *He works hard and follows all the rules at his job.* _____
2. _____
3. _____
4. _____
5. _____
6. _____
7. _____

B Find the words.

dependable	friendly	hardworking	responsible

d	i	h	l	a	t	i	l	a	o	r	z	l	l	r	y	q	m	s	l
n	l	j	d	t	r	e	s	p	o	n	s	i	b	l	e	y	n	o	v
y	i	c	d	i	k	l	g	g	g	y	d	k	w	m	i	o	d	t	y
g	s	t	v	r	e	o	i	r	b	h	w	w	t	s	j	t	p	w	c
a	u	j	n	x	c	f	r	i	e	n	d	l	y	q	s	r	a	z	l
c	k	n	d	d	j	z	n	s	a	c	v	l	g	h	z	s	h	u	g
e	h	k	s	u	u	q	w	t	o	d	e	p	e	n	d	a	b	l	e
h	p	e	o	b	y	k	e	i	c	y	k	u	u	t	d	n	m	a	i
b	s	d	h	a	r	d	w	o	r	k	i	n	g	u	p	k	h	a	c
q	d	u	g	q	z	t	b	l	p	q	p	f	h	p	m	t	h	i	j

C Talk with a partner. Answer the question. Make a list.

In your native country, what do you need to do to be a good employee?

© Cambridge University Press 2010   Photocopiable

Worksheet 27 Government leaders in the United States

A Read the article. Circle the answers.

Government Leaders in the United States

The president of the United States is the chief executive (leader) of the country and the commander in chief of the military. The vice president works with the president. The two parts, or branches, of Congress are the Senate and the House of Representatives. Congress makes laws for the United States. There are two U.S. senators from each state, but the number of U.S. representatives is different in each state.

Each state in the United States has a chief executive called a governor. Cities and towns also have chief executives called mayors. Many cities have a group of leaders called aldermen. Aldermen represent the people living in the city.

1. The leader of the country is the _____ .
   a.) president
   b. governor
   c. mayor
   d. vice president

2. There are two _____ from each state.
   a. mayors
   b. governors
   c. U.S. representatives
   d. U.S. senators

3. The leader of each state is the _____ .
   a. president
   b. governor
   c. mayor
   d. vice president

4. The leader of each city or town is the _____ .
   a. president
   b. governor
   c. mayor
   d. vice president

B Work with a partner. Answer the questions about current leaders in the U.S. government.

1. Who is the president? _____

2. Who is the vice president? _____

3. Who is the governor of your state? _____

4. Who are the U.S. senators from your state? _____

5. Who is one U.S. representative from your state? _____

6. Who is the mayor of your city or town? _____

7. Write the names of any other government leaders you know. _____

_____

© Cambridge University Press 2010   Photocopiable

Worksheet 28 *How can we help protect the environment?*

A Read the article. Match.

The environment is the world around us. There are many environmental problems. One problem is dirty air, or air pollution. Cars and factories put chemicals into the air. In some places, the air is not safe to breathe. Another environmental problem is wasting water. We use too much water every day. A third environmental problem is garbage. We throw away too much of it. The average person throws away about 4 pounds of trash per day. That is too much garbage!

What can we do about these problems? To make the air cleaner, we can drive our cars less, take the bus, ride a bicycle, or walk. To stop wasting water, we can take shorter showers. We can water our outdoor plants early in the morning or late at night when it is cooler. For the third problem, we can recycle instead of throwing things away. We can reuse (use again) items whenever it is possible.

Environmental problems

1. air pollution
2. water waste
3. garbage

What can we do about it?

a. We can recycle instead and reuse items.
b. We can drive less, take the bus, ride a bicycle, or walk.
c. We can take shorter showers and water outdoor plants early in the morning or late at night.

B Complete the puzzle.

ACROSS

1. We can _____ instead of throwing things away.
4. One problem is dirty air, or air _____ .
5. We can _____ items.

DOWN

2. The _____ is the world around us.
3. Wasting _____ is not using water well.

C Talk with a partner. Ask and answer the questions.

1. What else can you do to help the environment?
2. What household items can you recycle?

© Cambridge University Press 2010 **Photocopiable**

Worksheet 29 *What can I use as an ID card?*

A Read the conversation. Circle the answers.

Tatiana Hi, Carlos. I have a question for you about identification cards.

Carlos Oh yeah, what's that?

Tatiana In my native country, everyone has a national ID card. We don't have that here in the United States, right? What should I use?

Carlos No, we don't have a national ID card in the United States, but you can use a driver's license as an ID card. You can also use a permanent resident card.

Tatiana I'm a permanent resident. Can I get a driver's license?

Carlos Yes, of course. You can apply for one at the Department of Motor Vehicles. It's also called the DMV.

Tatiana OK. Thanks a lot.

1. Is there a national ID card in the United States?
   a. Yes, there is.
   b. No, there isn't.

2. What can Tatiana use for identification in the United States?
   a. a driver's license or a permanent resident card
   b. her native country's ID card

3. Can Tatiana get a U.S. driver's license?
   a. Yes, she can.
   b. No, she can't.

4. Where can Tatiana apply for a driver's license?
   a. She can apply for one at the Social Security office.
   b. She can apply for one at the DMV.

B Read. Complete the application for Roxana.

Roxana is filling out an application for a driver's license. Her full name is Roxana Isela Gomes. Roxana lives in Sarasota, Florida. Her address is 2456 Pine Street, Sarasota, Florida, 34230. Her eyes and hair are brown. She is 5 feet 3 inches tall. She weighs 105 pounds. She was born on August 22, 1985.

FLORIDA DRIVER'S LICENSE APPLICATION

Last Name __*Gomes*__ (1) First Name _____ (2) Middle Name _____ (3)

Date of Birth _____ (4 month) / _____ (day) / _____ (year)

Address _____ (5)

City _____ (6) State _____ (7) Zip Code _____ (8)

Hair Color _____ (9) Eye Color _____ (10)

Height _____ (11) Weight _____ (12)

Worksheet **30** *Money!*

A Look at the pictures. Write the words.

| a dime | a nickel | a penny | a five-dollar bill | a one-dollar bill | a quarter |

1. _____

2. _____

3. _____

4. _____

5. _____

6. _____

B Match.

1. a dime   a. four quarters
2. a nickel   b. ten cents
3. a quarter   c. five one-dollar bills
4. a penny   d. twenty-five cents
5. one dollar   e. five cents
6. five dollars   f. one cent

C Work with a partner. Complete the charts.

1¢ + 10¢	*11¢*
$1 + 5¢	
$5 + 25¢	
$1 + $5 + 1¢	
$5 + 10¢ + 5¢	

one dollar and twenty-five cents	$1.25
six dollars and ninety-five cents	
	$2.50
ten dollars and twenty cents	
	$12
fifteen dollars	

© Cambridge University Press 2010   **Photocopiable**

Worksheet 31 Sue's new home

A Read the paragraph. Underline the different types of homes.

Sue rents an <u>apartment</u> now, but she wants to buy a home. She doesn't know what kind of home she should buy. She is married, and she has two children. She and her husband looked at a townhouse in the city, a condominium in a large building, a mobile home, and a duplex. Her husband likes the mobile home because it can move easily to different places. Sue prefers the duplex. She likes the separate entrance and the neighborhood where it is located.

B Match the types of housing with the definitions.

1. apartment __d__
2. townhouse ____
3. condominium ____
4. duplex ____
5. mobile home ____

a. a house connected to other houses, usually in a city
b. a house that can move easily to different places
c. an apartment in a large building owned by the people living in it
d. a set of rooms for living in, often rented by a landlord to tenants
e. a house with two separate apartments, each with a separate entrance

C Interview your classmates. Ask and answer the questions. Complete the chart.

1. Do you prefer to own or rent your home? Why?
2. What is your favorite type of home? Why?

Name	Prefers to own or rent	Favorite type of home
Teresa	rent – landlord fixes and pays for problems	apartment – easy to clean

© Cambridge University Press 2010 Photocopiable

Worksheet **32** _Help with housing_

A Read the flyer. Answer the questions.

> **Do you need help with housing? The U.S. Department of Housing and Urban Development (HUD) can help you! HUD helps you:**
>
> - Buy a home: We can help you get a **mortgage** (money you borrow to buy a house), look for a house, and know your rights when you are buying a house.
> - Rent a home: We can help you get a home for **reduced** (less) rent.
>
> _How?_
> - We offer **subsidized housing**: We pay part of the rent to landlords. Then landlords offer reduced rent homes to low-income tenants.
> - We offer the Housing Choice Voucher Program (**Section 8**): You can find your own place and use the voucher (a piece of paper that is like money) to pay for all or part of your rent.
> - We can help you sell your home: We can help you get your home ready to sell.
> - We help you find housing, food, and job skills if you are **homeless**.
> - We help you **improve** your home (make your home better) if you own one.

1. How does HUD help people buy a home? _____

_____

2. How does HUD help people rent a home? _____

_____

3. How does HUD help the homeless? _____

_____

B Match the words with the definitions.

1. a mortgage
2. HUD
3. low-income
4. improve
5. subsidized housing
6. Section 8

a. The government pays part of the rent.
b. make better
c. Housing Choice Voucher Program
d. U.S. Department of Housing and Urban Development
e. people who do not make a lot of money
f. money you borrow to buy a home

C Look in a phone book or use the Internet. Answer the questions.

1. What are some local agencies that can help you with housing? _____

_____

2. How do they help with housing? _____

_____

© Cambridge University Press 2010 **Photocopiable**

Worksheet 33 *What's on the menu?*

A Look at the menu. Circle the answers.

Betty's Coffee Shop	
Breakfast specials	**Pastries**
Bagel with cream cheese $2.00	Cinnamon roll $1.50
2 eggs cooked any way with toast $5.00	Danish $1.25
3-egg cheese omelet with toast $6.00	Donut $1.00
Pancakes $4.50	Muffin $2.00
French toast $5.50	(blueberry or corn)
Beverages	
Coffee ...... $1.00 Milk $1.25	
Tea ...... $1.00 Juice ...... $1.50 (orange, apple, or tomato)	

1. What is the least expensive pastry?
   (a) donut
   b. Danish
   c. muffin
   d. cinnamon roll

2. What is the most expensive special?
   a. pancakes
   b. French toast
   c. 3-egg cheese omelet with toast
   d. 2 eggs cooked any way with toast

3. How much is a muffin and coffee?
   a. $2.00
   b. $3.00
   c. $3.25
   d. $3.50

4. How much are pancakes and juice?
   a. $5.75
   b. $6.00
   c. $6.50
   d. $7.00

B Read about nutrition. Answer the questions.

> You should eat a nutritious breakfast if you want to stay healthy. A good breakfast should not have too much sugar or fat, but it should provide protein, vitamins, and minerals. Foods high in protein include meat, eggs, dairy products, and beans. Fruits (including juices) and vegetables have a lot of vitamins and minerals. Many breakfast foods have a lot of sugar and fat, including pastries, pancakes, and French toast.

1. What are examples of food with a lot of protein?

   _____

2. What foods have a lot of vitamins and minerals?

   _____

3. Look at the menu in Exercise A. What can you order that is healthy?

   _____

© Cambridge University Press 2010   Photocopiable

Worksheet 34 — Achieving your goals

A Read. Answer the questions.

> In the United States, adult students can choose to enroll (sign up) at their local adult school to take English, job training, or computer classes. Adult students can also enroll at a community college and take noncredit courses or credit-bearing courses toward a certificate or an associate's degree. In California, Regional Occupational Programs help prepare adult students for jobs, further study, and technical training. There are similar educational and training programs in many other states.
>
> There are many opportunities for adults to get the education and training to reach their goals. To learn more about adult schools, community colleges, or Regional Occupational Programs, talk to your school's admission office and search in the phone book or on the Internet.

1. What are two types of schools or programs for adults? _____

2. What are two types of classes adults can take? _____

3. What are two ways to learn more about education and training programs for adults?

_____

B Read. Complete the application.

> Silvio Rivas is applying to NJ Community College. His address is 123 Lafayette Ave. Bloomfield, NJ 07003. His home phone number is (973) 555-1980. His date of birth is May 14, 1969. He is a permanent resident. He was born in Colombia, and his primary language is Spanish. He's applying for the fall term. He plans to study for a certificate in auto mechanics.

NJ Community College Application

Term (circle):   Fall   Spring
                  1

Name _____
         2 (first name)   3 (last name)

Address _____
       4 (street)   5 (city)   6 (state)   7 (zip code)

Home phone _____ Date of birth _____ / _____ / _____
                 8   9 (month) 10 (day) 11 (year)

Country of citizenship _____ Primary language _____
                            12   13

Certificate or degree applying for: _____
                                              14

C Talk with a partner. Ask and answer the questions.

1. What are your goals?
2. What education or training programs do you want to enroll in?

© Cambridge University Press 2010   **Photocopiable**

Worksheet 35 · *What's the best day care for my child?*

A Look at the ad. Answer the questions.

Little Angels Day Care • 456 Walnut Street

Are you looking for a great place to leave your children while you are at work? We have the answer for you! We have five caring childcare workers and assistants. There are a lot of educational toys for your child to play with. We have a large outdoor play area. We take all ages. Leave your child with us, and you can relax.

---

1. What's the name of the childcare facility? _____

2. How many childcare workers are there? _____

3. What ages can go to this childcare facility? _____

B Read the conversation. Complete the checklist.

Sara Hi, Rita. I just visited Little Angels Day Care on Walnut Street.

Rita What did you think about it?

Sara Well, I'm not sure.

Rita Was it clean?

Sara Yes, it was clean.

Rita Did you see a certificate that shows that the day care is licensed?

Sara No, I didn't.

Rita Were there separate spaces for children of different ages? And did you see a fire extinguisher?

Sara No, the children were all together. And I didn't see a fire extinguisher.

Rita Was there a place for children to play outside?

Sara Yes, but it was very small. The brochure said it was large.

Day-care Checklist

• Is the facility clean?	Yes ☐	No ☐
• Is there a certificate that says the place is licensed?	Yes ☐	No ☐
• Are there separate places for children of different ages?	Yes ☐	No ☐
• Is there a fire extinguisher?	Yes ☐	No ☐
• Is there a large outside play area?	Yes ☐	No ☐

C Talk with a partner. Ask and answer the questions.

1. Do you think this is a good childcare facility? Why or why not? _____

_____

2. What do you think are some good qualities for a day-care center? _____

_____

© Cambridge University Press 2010   Photocopiable

Worksheet 36 Special programs at my child's school

A Read the conversation. Circle the answers.

Olga Hi, Maria. I'm worried. I don't have enough money for my children's lunches.

Maria Do you know about the National School Lunch Program? You can get free meals for your children.

Olga Really? How can I do that?

Maria You have to fill out an application. You have to write down your income. Low-income families can get free or reduced-price meals for their children.

Olga Thank you. Are there any other special programs at the school?

Maria Do you know about Head Start?

Olga What's Head Start?

Maria It's a program for families with young children. Your child can go to preschool for free or for a reduced price. Parents can learn about school, health, nutrition, and how to be involved in your child's education.

Olga Thanks again.

1. Why is Olga worried?
   a. She doesn't have enough money for her children's lunches.
   b. She doesn't have enough money for her children's school.

2. How can Olga participate in the National School Lunch Program?
   a. She has to pay money.
   b. She has to fill out an application.

3. Who can get free or reduced-price meals for their children at school?
   a. low-income families
   b. teachers at the school

4. What does Head Start offer for young children?
   a. It offers free or reduced-price preschool.
   b. If offers money for school lunches.

B Look at the flyer. Complete the sentences.

> **National School Lunch Program and School Breakfast Program**
> Who is elgible (who meets the requirements to receive these services)?
> • Families that receive food stamps
> • Low-income children in a Head Start program
> • Homeless children
> • Migrant children (children who move from place to place because of their parents' jobs)

1. The National School Lunch and the _____ programs are for school children.

2. Eligible children are in a family that receives _____ stamps.

3. _____ children in a Head Start program are also eligible.

4. _____ and _____ children are eligible, too.

© Cambridge University Press 2010 Photocopiable

Worksheet 37 *911 Emergency!*

A Read the article. Circle *T* (true) and *F* (false). Correct the false sentences.

> **Tips for Calling 911 in an Emergency:**
> 1. Stay calm. Try to tell the operator what happened in a calm way.
> 2. The operator will ask where you are. Give the correct address.
> 3. Try to answer questions clearly and calmly. You can just say "yes" or "no" if you can't talk.
> 4. Follow all the instructions that the 911 operator gives you.
> 5. Don't hang up until the operator tells you to do so.

        calm
1. You should stay ~~excited~~ when you call 911 about an emergency.   T   Ⓕ

2. You should tell the 911 operator your correct address.   T   F

3. You should try to answer questions clearly and calmly.   T   F

4. You should not follow all instructions the 911 operator gives you.   T   F

B Read the conversation. Answer the questions.

Operator 911. How may I direct your call?
    Lisa My house is on fire!
Operator What's your address?
    Lisa 243 Pine Street.
Operator I'll connect you with the fire department.
    Lisa Thanks. Please hurry!
Operator Don't worry. The fire department will be there shortly.

1. What is Lisa's emergency? _____

2. What information does the operator ask Lisa for? _____

3. Who is coming to help Lisa? _____

C Look in a phone book or use the Internet. Complete the form.

> **Emergency Telephone Numbers for My Community**
>
> Police: _____ Fire Department: _____
>
> Poison Control: _____
>
> My neighbor: _____ Phone number: _____
>
> Hospital: _____ Phone number: _____
>
> Other important numbers: _____

© Cambridge University Press 2010   Photocopiable

Worksheet 38 *Get involved in community activities.*

A Look at the class catalog. Answer the questions.

City of Greenville
Parks and Recreation Program Guide and Class Catalog
Get involved in community classes and activities!
You will learn new skills, make new friends, and have a healthy lifestyle.

Class	Location	Price
Swimming lessons for all ages and skill levels	all city pools	$50 for 5 lessons
Arts and crafts	Randolph	$100 for 10 lessons
Karate	West Gym	$150 for 10 lessons

---

1. Why is it a good idea to take a class? _____

2. How much do swimming lessons cost? _____

3. Where can you take karate classes? _____

B Read the article. Answer the questions.

Do your kids feel tired or bored? Would they like to meet new friends and learn new skills? There are many opportunities for them to participate in extracurricular (outside of school) activities. Are they interested in sports? They can join a class that's offered by your city's parks and recreation department. These classes are offered at reduced prices.

Another option is the Girl Scouts or Boy Scouts. When your kids join these organizations, they learn new skills. They also participate in community service projects. Is money a problem? Your city's Police Athletic League is free! This organization is supervised by police officers. They help young people learn important life skills. All of these programs will help your child to have a more interesting and healthy lifestyle.

---

1. Are classes offered by the city expensive? _____

2. What can children learn in the Girl Scouts and Boy Scouts? _____

_____

3. Who supervises the Police Athletic League? _____

4. How much does the Police Athletic League program cost? _____

5. Why should children participate in programs like these? _____

_____

C Work with a partner. Look in a phone book or use the Internet. Ask and answer the questions.

1. What extracurricular activities are offered in your city?

2. What activities are you interested in for you or your children?

© Cambridge University Press 2010 Photocopiable

Worksheet 39 *How can Anna stop graffiti in her neighborhood?*

A Read the conversation. Circle the answers.

Jack Hi, Anna. What's the matter?

Anna I'm so tired of seeing graffiti in our neighborhood.

Jack Did you know that you can call community services about that? They will come and remove the graffiti.

Anna Really? How can I get the phone number?

Jack You can get it on the Internet. Search for "community services" in our city, and you'll see the number on the Web site.

Anna Thanks a lot, Jack. Now our neighborhood will look a lot better!

1. Why is Anna upset?

   a. There is graffiti in her neighborhood.

   b. There is trash in her neighborhood.

2. What does Jack suggest?

   a. Anna should call the police.

   b. Anna should call community services.

3. Where can Anna get the number?

   a. Jack told her the number.

   b. She can get it on the Internet.

4. Why does Anna want the graffiti removed?

   a. She wants her neighborhood to look better.

   b. She doesn't like the color.

B Look at the flyer. Answer the questions.

☎ **Community Services Department**

Graffiti Removal Program

Putting graffiti on public or private property is against the law. If you see someone doing it, call 911. If you see graffiti on a wall, call 555-CITY to report it. The city will remove the graffiti.

---

1. Is putting graffiti on public or private property against the law? _____

2. What number do you call if you see someone putting graffiti on a wall? _____

3. What number do you call if you see graffiti on a wall? _____

C Talk with a partner. Look in a phone book or use the Internet.

What is the number for community services in your community? _____

© Cambridge University Press 2010   **Photocopiable**

Community resources

Worksheet 40 *How can I volunteer in my community?*

A Work with a partner. Read the article. Ask and answer the questions.

> ### Help Others and Yourself – Volunteer!
> **Volunteer Opportunities in the Phoenix Area**
>
> - **Habitat for Humanity** – Are you good at building things? Help build homes for people in your community.
> - **Library volunteer** – Do you like books? Help your local library. Put books on the shelves in alphabetical order.
> - **Drum teacher needed** – Are you musical? The Boys and Girls Club is looking for a drum teacher for the next school year.
> - **Volunteer at your child's school** – Read to your child's class, or help with daily activities. Talk to your child's teacher about volunteer opportunities.

1. Which volunteer opportunity looks the most interesting to you? Why? _____

_____

2. Which volunteer opportunities involve working with children? _____

_____

3. Which volunteer opportunities require skills? _____

_____

B Read. Complete the time sheet.

> Larry McKenna is a volunteer at the Douglas Public Library. He shelves books, or puts books that people return back on the shelves. He has to put them back in alphabetical order. He volunteers at the library eight hours each week. He works different hours on each day. This was his schedule last week. On May 15th, he worked from 9 a.m. to 11 a.m. On May 17th, he worked from 9 a.m. to 12:15 p.m. On May 19th, he worked from 4 p.m. to 7 p.m.

Date	Time in	Name of volunteer	Time out	Total time
May 15th	9:00 a.m.	Larry McKenna	11:00 a.m.	2 hours

© Cambridge University Press 2010 **Photocopiable**

Worksheet **41** *How are schools organized in the United States?*

A Read the article. Complete the chart.

The Education System in the United States

Education in the United States is similar to that of many other countries. There are public schools and private schools. Public schools are funded by the government. Schools are divided into grades according to children's ages. Some children attend preschool programs, such as Head Start and pre-kindergarten (pre-K), before going to kindergarten. Preschool starts at age 2½ or 3. If children are younger than 3, their parents can send them to day care. Most children attend kindergarten when they are 5 years old.

Kindergarten is a part of elementary school. Elementary school consists of kindergarten through 5th grade in most states. After elementary school is middle school or junior high school. Middle school students are in grades 6 through 8. Junior high school students are in grades 7 through 9. They are usually 11–14 years old. After middle school or junior high school, students attend high school. High school is for children ages 14 through 18. Some students choose to continue their education after high school. They attend community colleges or universities. Another type of school is vocational school, where you can learn a specific job skill. There is also adult education, where students learn another language or get their general education diploma (GED) if they did not complete high school.

Level / Grade	Typical age
Day care	
	2½ or 3
	5–10
Junior high school	

Level / Grade	Typical age
High school	
	18 and up
Vocational school	
Adult education	

B Look in a phone book or use the Internet. Answer the questions.

1. What is the name of your local school district?
2. How are the students divided into grades in your local school district?

elementary school	grades
middle school / junior high school	grades
high school	grades

C Talk with a partner. Ask and answer the questions.

1. What are some other types of schools?
2. If you have children, what schools do they attend?

© Cambridge University Press 2010   Photocopiable

Worksheet 42 — *Larissa mails a package.*

A Read the conversation. Circle the answers.

Larissa Hi, Julie. Can you help me?

Julie Sure. What do you need?

Larissa I want to mail a package to my mom in Denver. I bought her a new dress for her birthday. How can I mail it?

Julie You can put it in a cardboard box at home, or you can get a box from the post office. You have to put a label, or a sticker, on the box with your mom's address on it. You also have to write your own address, or the return address, on the package.

Larissa Do I have to pay for the box?

Julie You don't have to. You can ship it by priority mail and pay a flat rate for the postage. The post office will give you a box or envelope for that.

Larissa What's a flat rate, and what's postage?

Julie Postage is the money you pay for mailing a letter or package. A flat rate is a set price you pay, no matter how heavy or light the package is.

Larissa Is that the best way to mail my package?

Julie You can ask at the post office or use the post office Web site. You can find out the cheapest or fastest way to send your package to your mom.

Larissa Thanks a lot. I'll go to the post office now.

1. What does Larissa want to do?
   a. She wants to mail a letter.
   b. She wants to mail a package.

2. Can Larissa put her present in a box at home?
   a. Yes, she can.
   b. No, she can't.

3. How can Larissa find the best way to send her package?
   a. She can ask at the post office.
   b. She can ask her mom.

4. What does Larissa have to put on the package?
   a. She has to put the price of the dress on it.
   b. She has to put her mom's address on it and her own address (the return address).

B Match the words with the definitions.

1. postage
2. label
3. post office
4. a flat rate
5. return address

a. a set price that you pay for a package, no matter the weight
b. money you pay for mailing a letter or package
c. a sticker with an address on it
d. a place where you can mail letters and packages
e. the address of the sender of the letter or package

C Talk with a partner. Ask and answer the questions.

1. Do you send letters and packages at the post office?
2. What other services are available at the post office?

© Cambridge University Press 2010 Photocopiable

Worksheet 43 — *Planning activities*

A Read the paragraph. Complete the calendar for the Gonzalez family.

> Next week is a busy week for the Gonzalez family. Arturo, Maria, and Patricia have different after-school activities. On January 6th, Arturo is playing in a hockey game at 6:00 p.m. Maria has ballet lessons on Tuesdays and Thursdays from 4:00 p.m. to 5:00 p.m. Patricia has soccer practice on Wednesdays from 5:00 p.m. to 7:00 p.m. Mr. Gonzalez has a Neighborhood Watch meeting on January 2nd at 8:00 p.m. Finally, Mr. and Mrs. Gonzalez want to go to a concert at the community center at 9:00 p.m. on January 7th.

January						
Sun.	Mon.	Tues.	Wed.	Thurs.	Fri.	Sat.
1	2	3	4	5	6 *6:00 p.m. Arturo, hockey game*	7

B Write the month and the dates for next week on the calendar. If you have children, write in times to read with your child. Then write in times to check your child's backpack.

Sun.	Mon.	Tues.	Wed.	Thurs.	Fri.	Sat.
—	—	—	—	—	—	—

C Talk with a partner. Share your calendar from Exercise B. Discuss the ways your calendars are similar or different. Then ask and answer the questions.

1. Do you usually plan your schedule in advance?
2. If you have children, do you usually plan a time to read with your child or check your child's backpack? Why or why not?

© Cambridge University Press 2010   Photocopiable

Worksheet **44** *Visiting the public library*

A Read the questions and answers. Write *T* for true and *F* for false.
Correct the false sentences.

Getting a Library Card – Frequently Asked Questions (FAQs)

1. How do I get a card?
   - Go to any library location. Bring a valid photo ID with your name on it (driver's license, food stamp card, bank card, military ID, etc.).
   - Bring proof of residency (proof of where you live) with your name on it.
   - Fill out an application. Your first library card is free.
   - The librarian will issue (give) you a card.
2. How many books or other items can I check out?
   - You can check out up to 25 items at one time. Ten of these items may be DVDs.

_T_ 1. You don't have to pay to get your first library card.

____ 2. You can only check out five items with your library card.

____ 3. You need a valid photo ID to get a library card.

____ 4. You will get your library card in the mail.

____ 5. You can check out ten DVDs at one time.

____ 6. You can get a card at any library location.

B Fill out the library card application. Use your own information.

Walnut County Public Library Card Application

First name: _____ Last name: _____
　　　　　　　　　　　1　　　　　　　　　　　　　　　　　　　　　　　　　　　2

Birth date: _____ / _____ / _____
　　　　　　　3 (month)　　　　　　(day)　　　　　　　(year)

Gender (circle one):　　　Male　　　Female
　　　　　　　　　　　　　　　　　　4

Street address: _____
　　　　　　　　　　　　　　　　　　　　　　　　5

City: _____ State: _____ Zip code: _____
　　　　　　　　　6　　　　　　　　　　　　　　　　　7　　　　　　　　　　8

County: _____
　　　　　　　　　9

Area code: _____ Phone number: _____
　　　　　　　10　　　　　　　　　　　　　　11

E-mail address: _____
　　　　　　　　　　　12

Proof of residency (driver's license, utility bill, or state ID): _____
　　　　　　　　　　　　　　　　　　　　　　　　　　　　　13

C Work with a partner. Look in a phone book or use the Internet. Answer the questions.

1. What is the address of the nearest public library in your community?
2. What days and hours is it open?
3. What services does it offer for adults? For children?

© Cambridge University Press 2010　**Photocopiable**

Worksheet 45 Iris asks for a parent-teacher conference.

A Read the note. Circle the answers.

May 18, 2009

Dear Mrs. Johnson,

I would like to schedule a parent-teacher conference with you. I am worried about my son. He says that he doesn't understand his homework. I would like to speak to you about this problem. I work from 8 a.m. to 4 p.m. every day of the week. Can I come to talk to you at 7:30 a.m. or 4:30 p.m. one day next week?

Thank you very much. My phone number is 555-9876.

Sincerely,

Iris Perez

---

1. Who wrote this note?
   a. Iris Perez
   b. Mrs. Johnson

2. What does Iris want?
   a. She wants to speak to the principal.
   b. She wants to have a parent-teacher conference with her son's teacher.

3. Why does she want to speak with the teacher?
   a. Her son doesn't understand his homework.
   b. Her son doesn't speak English.

4. When can Iris speak to the teacher?
   a. She can come at 7:30 a.m. or 4:30 p.m.
   b. She can come any time.

B Write a note to your child's teacher. Ask for a parent-teacher conference.

© Cambridge University Press 2010 **Photocopiable**

Worksheet 46 *Emergency shelters*

A Read. Answer the questions.

Emergency Shelters

Emergency shelters are for people who lose their homes in a hurricane, flood, earthquake, or other natural disaster. The American Red Cross and the Salvation Army provide temporary shelter for victims of natural disasters.

Florida has many hurricanes. Because of this, Florida has a system of emergency shelters. These shelters provide temporary homes to many people. There are currently 23 counties in Florida that have emergency shelters to protect people in case of a natural disaster. People in Florida are taught where the nearest emergency shelter is so that they can be prepared for a hurricane.

1. Who are the people that go to emergency shelters?

   _____

2. Which organizations help provide shelter for victims of natural disasters?

   _____

3. Why does Florida have a lot of emergency shelters?

   _____

4. Why are people in Florida taught where the nearest emergency shelter is?

   _____

B Circle the correct answers.

1. Victims of _____ stay in emergency shelters.
   a. robberies
   b. natural disasters

2. The American Red Cross and the Salvation Army provide _____ for victims of natural disasters.
   a. temporary shelters
   b. permanent shelters

3. There is a system of _____ in Florida.
   a. emergency shelters
   b. natural disasters

4. People in Florida are taught where _____ is so that they can be prepared.
   a. the biggest emergency shelter
   b. the nearest emergency shelter

C Look in a phone book or use the Internet. Answer the question.

What are the names and addresses of emergency or temporary shelters in your area?

Emergency shelter	Address
1.	
2.	

© Cambridge University Press 2010 **Photocopiable**

Worksheet 47 *Following directions*

A Look at the diagram. Write the directions.

| north | northeast | northwest | southeast | southwest |

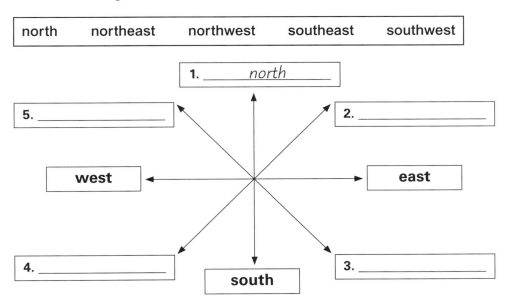

1. _____north_____

5. _____

2. _____

west ◄─────► **east**

4. _____

south

3. _____

B Look at the map. Then read the conversation with a partner. Draw Jim's route.

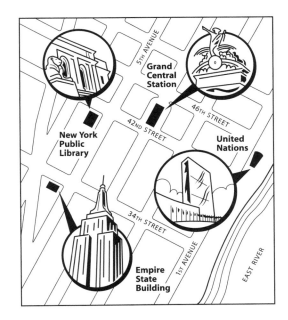

Jim Excuse me. How do I get to Grand Central Station?

Tom It's close to here. You're on Fifth Avenue and 34th Street now. Go north on Fifth Avenue to 42nd Street. Then turn right on 42nd Street. Walk east on 42nd Street to Grand Central Station. It will be on your left.

Jim OK, thanks! And where's the New York Public Library?

Tom It's also on 42nd Street. Walk west on 42nd Street from Grand Central Station. It will be on your left.

Jim Great! After I see Grand Central Station, I'll go to the Public Library.

C Write directions from school to your favorite place. Then tell a partner how to get to the place. Draw a map on a separate piece of paper to help your partner.

_____

_____

_____

© Cambridge University Press 2010   **Photocopiable**

Worksheet 48 *Public versus private health care*

A Read the article. Complete the chart.

Health Care in the United States

There are two types of health care for people living in the United States: private health care and public health care. Public health care is paid for by the U.S. government. Private health care is paid for by employers, individuals, or both.

These are some examples of public health-care programs that are funded by the U.S. government:

- **Medicare** – For U.S. citizens and residents 65 years and older
- **Medicaid** – For low-income people in certain categories, such as children, pregnant women, and disabled people with mental or physical disabilities
- **State Children's Health Insurance Program** – For low-income children who do not qualify for Medicaid
- **Veterans Administration** – Provides medical care to veterans (people who served in the military) and their families

---

Public health-care programs in the United States	Who is eligible (who can receive health care through this program)?
1. *Medicare*	*U.S. citizens and residents 65 years and older.*
2.	
3.	
4.	

B Match the words with the definitions.

1. public health care
2. private health care
3. veterans
4. health care
5. disabled people

a. people with mental or physical disabilities
b. medical care and services
c. health care that is paid for by the government
d. people who served in the military
e. health care that is paid for by employers or individuals

C Talk with a partner. Ask and answer the questions.

1. What do you think is good about public health care? What's bad about it?
2. What do you think is good about private health care? What's bad about it?

© Cambridge University Press 2010   **Photocopiable**

Worksheet 49 *Where can children get immunizations?*

A Read the conversation. Answer the questions.

Sara Hi, Randy. Did you register your children for school?

Randy Yes, I did.

Sara I still need to register my children.

Randy Do you have your children's immunization records?

Sara What are those?

Randy Papers that show that your children have gotten their shots, or immunizations.

Sara Oh. No, I don't have those. My children haven't gotten any shots. Where can I go for that?

Randy There's a public health clinic on Main Street. Your children can see a pediatrician and get immunizations for free.

Sara Great. I'll go there.

Randy They provide other services too, like prenatal care, or care for pregnant women.

Sara Thanks, Randy. I'll go home and look at the Web site. What's the name of the clinic? I'll call and make an appointment.

Randy It's Denver Public Health Clinic.

1. What do Sara's children need in order for her to register them? _____

2. Where can Sara go to get her children's immunizations? _____

3. Where is the clinic located? _____

4. What services does the Denver Public Health Clinic provide? _____

_____

B Look at the flyer. Answer the questions.

> **Denver Public Health Clinic**
> 445 N. Main St.
> Denver, Colorado 80220
>
> **Medical Services:**
> Immunizations
> Prenatal care
> Pediatric checkups
> (checkups for kids)

1. What is the address for the Denver Public Health Clinic? _____

_____

2. What medical services can you get there? _____

_____

3. What are pediatric checkups? _____

_____

C Work with a partner. Look in a phone book or use the Internet. Answer the questions.

1. What are some health-care providers in your community?

2. Are they public or private?

3. Where can you get prenatal care or immunizations in your community?

© Cambridge University Press 2010 Photocopiable

Worksheet **50** *Help Wanted*

A Read about help-wanted ads. Answer the questions.

> Are you looking for a job? There are many different ways to find a job. You can look in the Classified section of a local newspaper under "Employment." You can look on the Internet for jobs in your area. You can also look on bulletin boards at places in your community, such as your school or local businesses. Another way to look for a job is to ask your friends if they know about any job openings.

1. Write four places you can find ads for jobs.

   _____

   _____

2. What do you think is the best way to find a job? Why?

   _____

B Look at the ads. Circle *T* (true) or *F* (false). Correct the false sentences.

HELP WANTED!		
Orderly	**Auto mechanic**	**Cook**
University Hospital	Bob's Autos	Betty's Coffee Shop
P/T nights	F/T	P/T Mon.–Thur.
Exp. a plus	Need exp.	No exp. nec.
555-9876	555-4632	555-9988

　　　　　　　　　　　　　　　　　cook
1. Betty's Coffee Shop is looking for a ~~busboy.~~　　　　　　T　　Ⓕ

2. University Hospital needs a part-time orderly.　　　　　T　　F

3. Experience is not necessary for the auto mechanic job.　　T　　F

4. You need experience to work at Betty's Coffee Shop.　　T　　F

5. Call 555-8899 if you want to work at University Hospital.　T　　F

6. Call 555-4632 if you want to work at Bob's Autos.　　　T　　F

7. Betty's Coffee Shop needs someone to work on Monday or Thursday.　T　　F

8. Experience is a plus at University Hospital.　　　　　T　　F

C Talk with a partner. Ask and answer the questions.

1. Do you prefer part-time or full-time jobs? Why?
2. Do you prefer to work the day or the night shift? Why?

© Cambridge University Press 2010　Photocopiable

Worksheet 51 *How can I get a good job?*

A Read the article. Answer the questions.

> ### Five Steps to Getting a Job
>
> 1. Go to an employment center. At an employment center, you can look at job ads and speak to an employment counselor. An employment counselor can help you find a new job.
> 2. Write a resume. A resume is a paper with information about your work experience. It should include your contact information, your school, and your work experience.
> 3. Look at job ads in the newspaper and online.
> 4. Practice having an interview with a friend. Your friend can be the employer and ask you questions.
> 5. When you get an interview, be sure to dress professionally. Be friendly!

1. Why should you speak to an employment counselor? _____

2. What is a resume? _____

3. Where can you look for job ads? _____

4. What is one way to prepare for an interview? _____

B Read John's interview with an employment counselor. Answer the questions.

Counselor Good morning, John. Can you tell me a little about yourself?

John I'm attending English classes now at the community college.

Counselor Do you have experience working with children?

John Yes. I worked at a day-care center before I came to the United States.

Counselor Why do you want to be a childcare worker?

John I like working with children. I'm a friendly person. I think I will enjoy it.

Counselor OK. Well, I'll see what kinds of childcare jobs are available.

1. What is John's work experience? _____

_____

2. Why does he want to be a childcare worker? _____

_____

C Work with a partner. List three questions to ask an employment counselor.

1. _____

2. _____

3. _____

© Cambridge University Press 2010   Photocopiable

Worksheet 52 *Workers' rights*

A Read the article. Complete the paragraph.

> ## What Are Some Workers' Rights in the United States?
>
> **Workers have the right to:**
> - work in a safe workplace.
> - get a fair wage. Employers cannot pay less than the minimum wage – the minimum wage is the amount that employers must pay employees per hour. Employers must pay overtime (pay for extra hours) after workers have worked 40 hours in a week.
> - take a break after they work a certain amount of hours.
> - work if they have a disability. Employers cannot discriminate against hiring a worker with a disability.
> - work without facing discrimination because of age, gender (male or female), race, or religion.

disability	discrimination	minimum wage	overtime

> Ali found a new job at the hardware store. Now, he earns the
> _____ per hour. If he works _____ ,
>   1   2
> he gets paid more money per hour. Ali works in a wheelchair. He has a
> _____ . Ali got hired because he is a good worker. He can do
>   3
> his job as a cashier while he sits in his wheelchair. He has the right to work
> without _____ .
>   4

B Read about the agencies. Match the problem with the agency you can complain to.

> - **U.S. Equal Employment Opportunity Commission (EEOC)** – You cannot discriminate against someone because of their age, race, religion, gender, or disability.
> - **Occupational Safety and Health Administration (OSHA)** – You have the right to safe and healthy workplaces.

Problem	Agency
1. Your workplace is dirty and unsafe.	a. EEOC
2. You didn't get hired because of your age.	b. OSHA

© Cambridge University Press 2010 **Photocopiable**

Worksheet 53 | *Miguel's job application*

A Read about Miguel. Complete his job application.

Miguel is applying for a job. He saw an ad in the newspaper for a job as a cook in a restaurant. He is interested in this job because he used to be a cook in Mexico. Miguel's full name is Miguel Armando Vicente. His address is 21000 NW 15th Street, Miami, FL 33179. His social security number is 000-456-7890. His telephone number is (773) 555-9124. He wants to work full time, 40 hours per week. He can work days or nights, and he is available to begin work immediately.

At his last job in Mexico, Miguel was the main cook at "Restaurante Americano," where he cooked different kinds of American food. The address of this restaurant is 515 Calle Azul, Nogales, Sonora, Mexico. He worked at this restaurant from August 2006 to February 2009. He left the job because he moved to the United States with his family. It is OK to contact his last employer because Miguel is on good terms with his last supervisor, Jaime Mora.

APPLICATION FOR EMPLOYMENT

Name: _____*Miguel*_____ _____ _____
           1 (First)   2 (Middle)   3 (Last)

Address: _____
                                        4

Telephone number: _____
                                     5

Social Security Number: _____
                                          6

Position applied for: _____
                                      7

How many hours can you work weekly? _____ Can you work nights? _____
                                                          8   9

Full time or part time: _____
                                        10

When are you available to work? _____
                                                  11

WORK EXPERIENCE

Name of last supervisor: _____
                                                    12

Address: _____
                                      13

Employment dates: From _____ to _____
                                          14   15

Job duties: _____
                                  16

Reason for leaving: _____
                                      17

May we contact your last employer? _____
                                                      18

© Cambridge University Press 2010   **Photocopiable**

Worksheet 54 *The Bill of Rights*

A Read the article. Circle *T* (true) or *F* (false). Correct the false sentences.

The Bill of Rights

The **Constitution** of the United States of America is our nation's supreme law, or most important law. The first ten **amendments**, or changes, that were made to the U.S. Constitution are known as the **Bill of Rights**. These rights are given to people living in the United States. Here are descriptions of the ten amendments:

1. Freedom of religion: People can practice any religion that they want.
   Freedom of speech: People can say or print whatever they want.
   Freedom of assembly: You can meet peacefully with a group of people.
2. People can have weapons or own a gun (within the limits of the law).
3. The U.S. government cannot force people to keep soldiers in their homes during times of peace.
4. The government cannot search your house or property without a court order.
5. A person cannot be tried twice for the same crime.
   A person cannot be forced to testify, or be a witness, against himself.
6. If you are charged with a crime, you have the right to a trial and a lawyer.
7. If you are charged with a crime, you have the right to a trial by jury.
8. The government cannot charge fines that are too high.
9. People have more rights that are not in the Constitution.
10. If the Constitution does not give a power to the U.S. government, that power belongs to the state or to the people.

---

         first
1. The Bill of Rights is the ~~last~~ ten amendments to the U.S. Constitution.   T   (F)

2. Freedom of speech is part of the first amendment.   T   F

3. The fifth amendment states that a person can be tried twice for the same crime.   T   F

4. If you are charged with a crime, you have the right to have a lawyer.   T   F

5. People have rights that are not in the Constitution.   T   F

B Answer the questions.

1. What is freedom of religion? _____

2. What is freedom of speech? _____

3. What is freedom of assembly? _____

C Talk with a partner. Ask and answer the questions.

1. What makes the Bill of Rights so important?
2. Which amendment do you think is most important? Why?

© Cambridge University Press 2010   **Photocopiable**

Worksheet 55 *The three branches of the U.S. government*

A Read the article. Circle the answers.

The Three Branches of Government

There are three branches of government in the United States. They are the executive, legislative, and judicial branches. The president and the vice president are the leaders of the country. They form the executive branch of the government. They are both elected, or chosen, in November every four years.

The legislative branch of the United States is called Congress. The members of Congress make laws. Congress has two parts: the Senate and the House of Representatives. There are 100 U.S. senators – two from each of the 50 states in the United States. There are 435 U.S. representatives, but the number of representatives is different for each state. Americans elect U.S. senators for six-year terms and U.S. representatives for two-year terms.

The third branch of the government is the judicial branch. The judicial branch is the Supreme Court. There are nine Supreme Court justices (judges). They review and explain laws. Presidents choose Supreme Court justices, and they have terms for life.

1. We elect the president for _____ years.
   a. 2
   (b.) 4
   c. 6

2. Congress _____ .
   a. leads the country
   b. reviews and explains laws
   c. makes laws

3. There are _____ U.S. senators.
   a. 9
   b. 100
   c. 435

4. We elect U.S. senators for _____ years.
   a. 2
   b. 4
   c. 6

5. There are _____ U.S. representatives.
   a. 50
   b. 100
   c. 435

6. We elect U.S. representatives for _____ years.
   a. 2
   b. 4
   c. 6

7. There are _____ Supreme Court justices.
   a. 4
   b. 6
   c. 9

8. Supreme Court justices _____ .
   a. lead the country
   b. review and explain laws
   c. make laws

B Talk with a partner. Describe the similarities and differences between your native country's system of government and the United States' system of government.

© Cambridge University Press 2010   Photocopiable

Worksheet 56 *How can I contact my state's elected officials?*

A Read the conversation. Answer the questions.

Rita I'm so upset! My daughter's teacher lost her job today. The school district is trying to save money because of state budget cuts.

Sam What are budget cuts?

Rita That's when the state has to spend less money on government programs. Because of that, the schools have less money, so they spend less money on teachers.

Sam That's terrible!

Rita I want to do something about it. But what?

Sam You could contact the governor.

Rita How do I contact my governor?

Sam You can use the Internet to find the name and e-mail address of the governor.

1. Why is Rita upset? _____

2. What does Sam suggest that Rita do? _____

3. How can Rita find her governor's contact information? _____

B Read Rita's e-mail. Circle *T* (true) or *F* (false). Correct the false sentences.

> Dear Governor:
>
> I am writing because I am concerned about my daughter's education. Her teacher lost her job because of budget cuts. My daughter's school won't have art and music teachers next year. We need all of these excellent teachers. Please consider giving more money to our schools.
>
> Sincerely,
> Rita Sanchez

daughter's
1. Rita is concerned about her ~~son's~~ education.   T   (F)

2. Her daughter's teacher lost her job because of budget cuts. T   F

3. The school will have art and music teachers next year.   T   F

4. Rita thinks the school needs all of the teachers.   T   F

5. Rita wants the governor to give more money to the schools.   T   F

C Work with a partner. Answer the questions.

1. Who is your state governor?
2. How can you find his/her contact information?

© Cambridge University Press 2010   Photocopiable

Worksheet 57 IDs and documents for transportation

A Read about Jane Mason. Complete her driver's license.

> Jane Mason's date of birth (DOB) is 09-15-58. She does not need a new driver's license until her driver's license expires on 01-01-13. Her address is 960 Water Street, Chicago, IL 60611. She is 5' (feet) 3" (inches) tall, and she weighs 110 lbs (pounds). Her eyes are brown.

ILLINOIS   **DRIVER'S LICENSE**

Lic. No.: **D123 - 4567 - 8910**
DOB: _0 9_ - _1 5_ - _5 8_
Expires: __ __ - __ __ - __ __
Issued: **0 8 - 1 3 - 0 8**

_____ (name)   Class: D
_____ (street address)   Type: ORG
_____ (city, state, zip code)

Jane Mason

Female _____ ' _____ " inches _____ lbs _____ eyes

B Read about Jane's documents. Circle the answers.

> Jane needs documents when she drives. She always keeps her registration and insurance cards in her car. When a police officer stops Jane, she has to show her driver's license, registration, and insurance. Without these documents, the police officer will give her a traffic ticket. Drivers get traffic tickets when they break traffic laws.
>
> Jane also needs documents when she travels to another country. She needs to take her passport, which shows her nationality or citizenship. A passport is required to enter and leave the United States.

1. What does Jane always keep in her car?
   a. her passport
   b. her insurance card
   c. her credit card

2. What does Jane have to show a police officer?
   a. license, insurance, and passport
   b. license, insurance, and registration
   c. insurance, registration, and passport

3. When do drivers get traffic tickets?
   a. when they don't have their passports
   b. when they travel to another country
   c. when they break traffic laws

4. What does Jane need to travel to another country?
   a. a passport
   b. a registration card
   c. an insurance card

© Cambridge University Press 2010   Photocopiable

Worksheet 58 · *American holidays*

A Read. Complete the chart.

Americans celebrate national holidays throughout the year. In January, Americans celebrate Martin Luther King Jr. Day. He is remembered for his peaceful fight for equal rights for all Americans. In February, Americans celebrate Presidents' Day. This holiday celebrates the first president, George Washington, and the sixteenth president, Abraham Lincoln, who united the United States after the Civil War. On Memorial Day, in May, Americans remember soldiers who died in military service. July 4th is Independence Day. This day celebrates the birthday of the United States. There are often celebrations with fireworks and parades.

On Labor Day in September, Americans celebrate all workers. In October, Americans remember Christopher Columbus. He introduced Europeans to America. Veterans Day is usually celebrated on November 11th. People who were in the military are remembered. Thanksgiving is also in November. It celebrates a time when Native Americans shared a large meal with British colonists. Families and friends get together and have a large dinner – usually with a turkey.

1. *Martin Luther King Jr. Day*	*People remember Martin Luther King, Jr., for his peaceful fight for equal rights for all Americans.*
2.	
3.	
4.	
5.	
6.	
7.	
8.	

© Cambridge University Press 2010   **Photocopiable**

Worksheet 59 *Voting in the United States*

A Read the article. Answer the questions.

Voting in the United States

It is a right and responsibility to vote in the United States. Voting gives you a voice. When you vote, you elect, or choose, your government representatives. If you are a U.S. citizen and are 18 or older, you can vote in the United States. Before you can vote, you have to register (in all states except for North Dakota).

In the United States, most of our elected officials come from the two largest **political parties**. These are the **Democratic** and **Republican** parties.

One of the most important elections in the Unites States is for the president. The first election is called the **primary election**. That is when people vote for candidates from their political parties to run for president. After that, the presidential candidates each choose a vice-presidential candidate. Finally, on **Election Day**, in November, people vote for a presidential candidate in the **general election**. The candidate who wins the election becomes president.

---

1. What is one reason it is important to vote? _____

2. Who can vote in the United States? _____

3. What are the two biggest political parties in the United States? _____

4. What is the primary election? _____

5. When is Election Day? _____

B Complete the puzzle.

ACROSS

1. _____ Day is in November.

5. The two major political parties in the United States are the Republican and _____ parties.

6. In the _____ election, one candidate from each political party is chosen to run for president.

DOWN

2. You must be _____ years old to vote in the United States.

3. It is a right and responsibility to _____ in the United States.

4. There are two or more presidential _____ in the general election for the presidency.

© Cambridge University Press 2010   Photocopiable

Worksheet 60 — *Where do you live?*

A Look at the map. Circle your state.

B Answer the questions.

1. What state do you live in? _____

2. What is the capital of your state? _____

3. What is the capital of the United States? _____

C Work with a partner. Look at the map. Write the names of the countries and oceans.

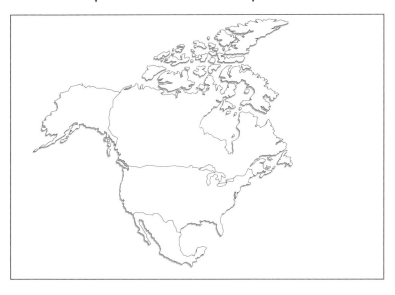

History and government

© Cambridge University Press 2010 **Photocopiable**

Worksheet **61** *Satisfaction guaranteed?*

A Read the article. Circle *T* (true) or *F* (false). Correct the false sentences.

Writing a Letter of Complaint

Have you ever been unhappy or dissatisfied with something you bought, or a service you received? One way to deal with dissatisfaction over a product or service is to write a letter of complaint. Here are some suggestions:

1. Address the letter to someone with authority to fix the problem.
2. If you are dissatisfied with a product, state when and where you bought it. Also include the name and model number of the product, the serial number, and a copy of the receipt. Keep the original receipt.
3. If you are complaining about service, state the problem briefly. Include dates and times when the incident happened.
4. Say what you want – a refund or exchange, or just an apology.
5. Be sure to include your name, address, and phone number.
6. Keep a copy of everything you send.

---

1. Writing a letter of complaint is one way to deal with <u>*dis*satisfaction</u>   T   (F)
   over a product or service.

2. Send the original receipt of the product you bought with your   T   F
   letter of complaint.

3. If you are complaining about service, be sure to include the date   T   F
   and time of the incident.

4. In the letter, say what you would like from the company.   T   F

5. It is not necessary to keep a copy of everything you send.   T   F

B Read the letter. It is missing information. Work with a partner to rewrite the letter on a separate piece of paper. Use the article in Exercise A to help you.

Dear Mr. Smith:

   I purchased a set of dinner plates from your company on January 2, 2009. When the plates arrived in the mail, many of them were broken. I am very upset and will not buy anything from your company again.

                                          Sincerely,
                                          Peter Johnson
                                          Peter Johnson

© Cambridge University Press 2010   Photocopiable

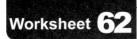

Worksheet 62 *Omar's starting a new business.*

A Read the conversation. Number the steps in the correct order.

Brian Hi, Omar. How's it going?

Omar Fine. My wife and I are thinking about starting our own business.

Brian Really? What kind of business?

Omar We're thinking about opening up a shop. We want to sell jewelry and clothing.

Brian That's a great idea!

Omar I've been researching ways to start my own business.

Brian What do you have to do?

Omar First, we need to write a business plan. A business plan will help us to know how we're going to sell our products and run our business.

Brian OK. Then what?

Omar Then we'll have to look at the market for our business – you know, find out if people here are interested in buying our jewelry and clothing.

Brian I see. And after that?

Omar We'll have to get a license, or a permit, to sell our products and think of a name.

Brian Great! Anything else?

Omar We'll have to find out how to file taxes for our own business. We'll also have to get business insurance and a loan to rent the space for the store.

Brian Do you know where the store will be?

Omar Right now we're trying to find a good place.

Brian Good luck! I'll come to your shop when you open for business.

Omar's eight steps to starting his own business

_____ Find a good place for the shop.

_____ Think of a name for the business.

_____ Get a license or permit.

_1_ Write a business plan.

_____ Find out about business taxes.

_____ Get a loan from the bank.

_____ Find out if people are interested in buying the product.

_____ Get business insurance.

B Match the words with the definitions.

1. loan   a. a plan for running a business

2. license   b. money you borrow from the bank

3. products   c. a permit to sell products

4. business plan   d. what you will sell in your business

C Talk with a partner. Ask and answer the questions.

1. Would you like to have your own business?

2. What kind of business would you like to have?

© Cambridge University Press 2010   Photocopiable

Worksheet 63 Rental agreements

A Complete the sentences.

| landlord | lease | refunded | security deposit | tenants |

Rosa is the owner, or _____*landlord*_____ , of an apartment building near
San Diego. She rents apartments in the building to _____ .
Tenants have to sign a _____ , or rental agreement. It says what
the tenant needs to pay each month for rent and how long the tenant agrees to
stay in the apartment. Also, tenants usually pay a _____ when
they rent an apartment. This is money given to the landlord for protection against
damages. The money is given back, or _____ , when tenants move
out if the apartment is not damaged and is in good condition.

B Read the paragraph. Use the information in the paragraph to complete the
rental agreement.

> John Marks has decided to rent an apartment in his building to a new
> tenant named Sarah Smith. John, the landlord, will rent the apartment to her
> from May 1, 2009, to April 30, 2010. Sarah needs to pay a security deposit of
> $400 when she signs the rental agreement. She will then pay $800 in rent on
> the first day of every month. She will also pay for gas and electricity, but John
> will pay for heat and water.

Rental Agreement – Sunrise Apartments

The landlord, ____*John Marks*____ , and the tenant, _____ ,
agree to the following:

- The landlord rents the property to the tenant for these dates:

  _____ to _____ .

- The tenant will pay the following security deposit: _____ .

- The monthly rent is _____ , due on the

  _____ day of every month.

- The tenant agrees to pay for gas and _____ . The landlord

  agrees to pay for heat and _____ .

© Cambridge University Press 2010   Photocopiable

Worksheet 64 *Guarantees, warranties, and complaints*

A Read the story. Circle *T* (true) or *F* (false). Correct the false sentences.

> Yesterday, Jon bought a new large-screen TV. The TV has a guarantee to last for two years. Jon also bought an extended warranty with the TV for one more year. With the extended warranty, the store will fix or give him a new TV if it breaks up to one year after the guarantee expires (ends).
>
> When Jon brought the TV home, he set it up right away. He noticed that the TV had problems. The picture faded in and out – it became less clear and then disappeared. Tomorrow Jon is going to take the TV back to the store. He will bring the TV, original receipt, guarantee, and extended warranty. He is sure that the store will refund (or give back) his money or exchange his TV for a new one.

two
1. The TV has a guarantee to last for ~~three~~ years.　　　　T　　Ⓕ

2. The extended warranty is good for two years after the　　T　　F
   guarantee expires.

3. Jon will bring the TV, original receipt, guarantee, and　　T　　F
   extended warranty to the store.

4. Jon is not sure that the store will refund his money.　　T　　F

B Complete the conversation. Then practice the conversation with a partner.

| exchange | guarantee | receipt | refund | warranty |

Jon Hi. I have a complaint. I bought this TV here yesterday, but it doesn't work.

Salesperson What's the problem?

Jon The picture fades in and out.

Salesperson Do you have the original _____*receipt*_____ ?
　　　　　　　　　　　　　　　　　　　1

Jon Yes. Here it is.

Salesperson I see you have a two-year _____ . You also bought an
　　　　　　　　　　　　　　　　　　　　2
extended _____ on the TV for one more year. Do you
　　　　　　　　　　3
want a _____ , or do you prefer to _____ this TV
　　　　　　　　4　　　　　　　　　　　　　　5
for a different one?

Jon I want a different one. Can you show me some other TVs?

Salesperson Sure. Come with me.

© Cambridge University Press 2010　**Photocopiable**

Worksheet 65 *Landlord and tenant rights*

A Match the words with the definitions.

1. to evict __d__
2. tenant ____
3. landlord ____
4. lease ____

   a. an agreement or contract to rent a property
   b. a person who owns and rents a property to other people
   c. a person who pays rent to live in a property
   d. to force a person to leave a property

B Read the article. Answer the questions.

> ## Landlords and Tenants
> ### Frequently Asked Questions (FAQs)
>
> **1. What are the responsibilities of a tenant?**
> - Pay the rent on time.
> - Keep the property clean.
> - Tell the landlord if there is a problem with the property.
> - Do what he or she has agreed to do in the lease.
> - Give the landlord advance notice before moving out.
>
> **2. What are the responsibilities of a landlord?**
> - Be sure that the home is safe for the tenant to live in.
> - Give advance notice before entering the tenant's home, unless there is an emergency.
> - Give the tenant written notice before ending the lease.
>
> **3. When can a landlord evict a tenant?**
> - The tenant does not pay the rent.
> - The tenant damages the property.
> - The lease expires (comes to an end), and the tenant does not leave.
> - The tenant does not do the things he or she agreed to do in the lease.

1. If there is a problem with the property, what should a tenant do?

   A tenant should tell the landlord if there is a problem with the property.

2. What should a tenant do before moving out?

   _____

3. When can a landlord enter a tenant's home without giving advance notice?

   _____

4. What happens if a tenant does not pay the rent?

   _____

5. What are two other reasons that a landlord can evict a tenant?

   _____

© Cambridge University Press 2010   Photocopiable

Worksheet 66 *Sara's family budget*

A Edith and Sara are talking about budgets. Read their conversation with a partner. Match the words with the definitions.

Edith What's the matter, Sara?

Sara I'm worried about money. Even though my husband and I both work hard, we spend all of the money we earn on our expenses. I don't like **living paycheck to paycheck**, and I shouldn't use my credit card.

Edith Have you thought about setting up a **family budget**?

Sara A family budget? What do you mean?

Edith It's a plan to help you understand how your family spends money so you can save money. First, you have to write your **net income** – the money you earn after taxes – and all your **expenses**. You should write everything, from the amount of money you spend on rent to the amount of money you spend on **entertainment** – movies, concerts, things like that. Add everything up, and look at the difference between your monthly net income and your expenses. Then, look at your expenses and think about what you can do to spend less on them.

Sara I like that idea. How can I start?

Edith I can show you a chart that I use to make our family budget.

Sara Thanks for your help!

1. net income *e*
2. family budget _____
3. expenses _____
4. entertainment _____
5. living paycheck to paycheck _____

a. ways of enjoying yourself
b. money you spend
c. spending your entire income on expenses
d. helps families save money
e. money earned after taxes

B Look at Sara's family budget. Answer the questions.

Monthly net income		Monthly expenses			
Sara	$1,100	Rent:	$1,000	Cell phone:	$50
Jim	$1,400	Utilities:	$200	Clothing:	$125
		Food:	$600	Entertainment:	$100
		Car, gas, insurance:	$600		
Total: $2,500		Total: $2,675			

1. What is Sara and Jim's total monthly net income? ___$2,500___

2. How much money in total do they spend each month? _____

3. What is the difference between their monthly net income and expenses? _____

4. How much money do they spend monthly on clothing and entertainment? _____

C Sara and Jim want their monthly net income to be more than their monthly expenses. Talk with a partner about what they can do to spend less.

Consumer economics

© Cambridge University Press 2010   Photocopiable

Name: _____

Worksheet 67 *How do I get there?*

A Look at the bus schedule. Answer the questions.

Monday thru Friday Northbound	Harrison/Wells (Main Post Office)	State/Chicago (Chicago History Museum)	Clark/Diversey (Lincoln Park Zoo)	Broadway/ Waveland	Broadway/Foster	Clark/Devon (Loyola University)
Bus A	8:01 a.m.	8:16 a.m.	8:33 a.m.	8:43 a.m.	8:55 a.m.	9:07 a.m.
Bus B	8:11	8:26	8:43	8:53	9:05	9:17
Bus C	8:21	8:36	8:53	9:03	9:15	9:27

1. Which bus leaves Clark and Diversey at 8:53 a.m.? ___*Bus C*___

2. What time does Bus A leave State and Chicago? _____

3. Which bus arrives at Clark and Devon at 9:17 a.m.? _____

4. How long does it take to get from Harrison and Wells to Clark

    and Devon? _____

5. How long does it take to get from Broadway and Waveland to Broadway

    and Foster? _____

B Look at the map. Answer the questions. Use north, south, east, or west.

1. How do you get from Millennium Park to the Ford Center?
    Walk north on N. Michigan Ave.
    Then walk west on W. Randolph St.

2. How do you get from the Ford Center to the John Hancock Observatory?

    _____

    _____

3. How do you get from the John Hancock Observatory to the Museum of Contemporary Art?

    _____

    _____

4. How do you get from the Museum of Contemporary Art to the Ford Center?

    _____

    _____

© Cambridge University Press 2010   Photocopiable

Community resources

Ventures Civics   **67**

Worksheet **68** *Be safe on the road!*

A Look at the flyer. Answer the questions.

> ## Be Safe on the Road!
> - Wear a seat belt at all times (the driver and all passengers).
> - Get a lot of rest before driving.
> - Don't take medicine or drink alcohol before driving.
> - Don't eat, drink, or talk on the phone while driving.
> - Be an alert driver. Stay aware of what is happening on the road.
> - Stop every two hours to take a break.
> - Reduce stress by planning your driving route, bringing directions, and allowing plenty of time for driving.

1. Who should wear seat belts in the car? _____*the driver and all passengers*_____

2. What should you do before driving? _____

3. What should you *not* do before driving? _____

4. What should you *not* do while driving? _____

5. What does an alert driver do? _____

6. How often should you take a break? _____

7. How can you reduce stress while driving? _____

_____

B Read the article. Match the words with the definitions.

> ## Don't Drink and Drive!
>
> What are the consequences of driving under the influence of alcohol (DUI)? There are many. If you are driving and a police officer pulls you over because he or she believes that you have been drinking, the police officer will test your blood alcohol content (BAC). If it is at or higher than the legal BAC limit for your state, you can be arrested. Other consequences include having your driver's license taken away, paying fines, or going to jail. If you drink when you are out with a group, take turns being the "designated driver." The designated driver doesn't drink. He or she drives everyone in the group home that night.

1. DUI _*b*_
2. designated driver ____
3. consequences ____
4. BAC ____

a. the results of an action
b. driving under the influence of alcohol
c. blood alcohol content
d. the person who doesn't drink and is the driver for a group of people

© Cambridge University Press 2010   Photocopiable

Worksheet 69 — Schools in the United States and in your native country

A Read the story. Answer the questions.

Francois Jardin and his family moved from Paris, France, to Seattle, Washington a few years ago. When Francois was younger, he attended Ronald Johnson Elementary School. Now, Francois is 12 years old and in the 7th grade. He attends Richland Middle School in Seattle. After Francois finishes 8th grade, he plans to attend the local high school for four years. When he graduates from high school, he wants to go to Seattle Community College and get an Associate's Degree. Then, he might transfer to the University of Washington.

Francois attends Richland Middle School because he lives in that school district. A district is a certain area of a city or town. Francois's father is a teacher in the same school district, at Ronald Johnson Elementary School. He is also on the school board at his school. School board members are elected to make decisions about the schools in their district. They also talk about the goals of the school.

1. What type of school does Francois attend? What grade is he in?

_____

2. What type of school will Francois attend after high school? What degree will he receive?

_____

3. What is a school district?

_____

4. What does the school board do?

_____

B Work with a partner. Complete the chart.

Type of school (U.S.)	Type of school (native country)	Type of school (partner's native country)
Elementary		
Middle school		
High school		
Community college / college		

C Talk with a partner. Ask and answer the questions.

1. What do you think is good about schools in your native country?
2. What is good about schools in the United States?

© Cambridge University Press 2010   Photocopiable

Worksheet 70 *Problems with medical insurance coverage*

A Read the conversation. Answer the questions.

Natalia Hi, Brisa. What's the matter?

Brisa My health insurance company won't pay for my son's asthma medication.

Natalia Can't you call the insurance company? You can tell them your son really needs the medication for his asthma, and then send a copy of the prescription.

Brisa That's a good idea. But who do I call?

Natalia Look on the back of your insurance card. It should have a telephone number you can call.

Brisa OK, I'll try that. Thanks for your help.

1. Why is Brisa upset? _____

2. What does Natalia suggest that Brisa do? _____

3. Where can Brisa find the number to call for the insurance company? _____

B Read the brochure. Circle the answers.

---

7 Steps You Can Take When You Have Problems with Medical Insurance Coverage

1. Find the paperwork that shows your insurance company's policies for medical expenses.
2. Read it carefully. Make sure you highlight, or circle, the policies that concern you.
3. Make copies of all your related prescriptions, doctor's notes, and medical bills.
4. Call the customer service number of your insurance company.
5. Tell the representative your problem.
6. Write down the date and time that you called, the full name of the person(s) you spoke with, and what happened in the conversation.
7. If nothing happens, try again. Ask to speak to the representative's supervisor.

---

1. What should you do first?
   a. Call the customer service number.
   b. Find the paperwork from your insurance company.

2. What copies should you make?
   a. copies of prescriptions, doctor's notes, and bills
   b. copies of a description of the problem

3. What should you write down when you speak to a representative?
   a. the person's name, the date, and the time
   b. the number you are calling

4. What if nothing happens?
   a. Try again. Then write an angry letter.
   b. Try again. Then ask to speak to the supervisor.

© Cambridge University Press 2010   Photocopiable

Health

Worksheet 71 — Substance abuse

A Read the paragraphs. Match the words with the definitions.

> What is **substance abuse**? It is using substances like drugs and alcohol in a way that is **harmful** (bad) for your body. Many people become **addicted** to drugs and alcohol. That means they cannot stop using these substances. They take the substances to change their mood (the way they feel). Often, the substances used are **illegal drugs**. The reason these drugs are illegal is that they are addictive and can cause negative, or bad, health effects. Use of these illegal substances is very dangerous and against the law.
>
> What are some reasons that people turn to substance abuse? Sometimes people do it to feel better, or there is a history of addiction in the family. Other times people feel **peer pressure**. This means that if other people around them are doing drugs, they can feel like they have to take them, too. This happens especially to teenagers.

1. peer pressure
2. substance abuse
3. harmful
4. addicted
5. illegal drugs

a. drugs that you can't get legally from a pharmacy
b. pressure to do something others around you are doing
c. You cannot stop doing something.
d. using substances like drugs and alcohol in a bad way
e. bad for you

B Read the phone conversation. Answer the questions.

Dirk This is the substance abuse hotline. How can I help you?

Ana I'm really worried about my friend. I think she might have an addiction problem.

Dirk What's going on with her?

Ana She's different than usual. She drinks a lot of alcohol, even on work days.

Dirk Have you noticed any other changes?

Ana Well, she forgets to do important things, like pay her bills or buy groceries.

Dirk The first step would be to talk to a substance abuse counselor. She or he can give you advice on how to help your friend. The counselor can refer you to substance abuse centers in your area. Here's the number: 555-1234.

Ana Thanks. I'll do that.

1. Why did Ana call the substance abuse hotline? _____

2. What changes has Ana noticed in her friend? _____

3. What does Dirk suggest? _____

C Look in a phone book or use the Internet. Answer the questions.

1. What is a place in your community that helps with substance abuse?

2. What is the address and phone number?

© Cambridge University Press 2010 Photocopiable

Worksheet 72 *Finding out about job opportunities*

A Look at the ad for a job fair. Circle *T* (true) or *F* (false). Correct the false sentences.

> **HOSPITALITY & FOOD SERVICE JOB FAIR**
> **Freedom Convention Center**
> March 12, 2010
> 45 employers! Free admission!
> **Don't miss out! Register by March 11th.**
> Call 239-555-7590.
> Must be 21 or older.
> Bring copies of your resume.

1. The job fair is on March ~~21~~ 12, 2010.   T   (F)

2. Thirty-five employers will be at the job fair.   T   F

3. There is no fee for admission.   T   F

4. Call 239-555-7509 to register.   T   F

5. Twenty-year-olds can come to the job fair.   T   F

6. The job fair is good for people who want to work in restaurants.   T   F

B Look at the help-wanted ad. Then complete the conversation with a partner.

> **Assistants needed**
> Lakewood Retirement Home
> No experience is necessary – we will train you!
> Day and night shifts available
> Fill out an application today! Call 520-555-8763.

assistants	experience	fill out	night	train

A Hello, this is Lakewood Retirement Home.

B Hi. My name is Sam Waters. I saw a help-wanted ad on the Internet for

  ___assistants___ at the Lakewood Retirement Home.
  1

A Oh, yes. You can come in and _____ an application at any time. Do
                                      2

  you have _____ ?
              3

B No, I don't.

A That's OK. We will _____ you. Are you available to work the
                            4

  _____ shift?
      5

B Yes, I am – on Mondays, Wednesdays, and Fridays.

A Good. We look forward to meeting you.

© Cambridge University Press 2010   Photocopiable

Worksheet 73 *Job interview questions and answers*

A Talk with a partner. Ask and answer the questions.

1. Have you ever had a job interview in the United States?
2. If you answered "yes," what kinds of questions did the interviewer ask you?

B Work with a partner. Match the job interview questions with the answers.

1. Do you have any experience doing this type of work? __e__
2. Why are you interested in this job? ____
3. What were your responsibilities at your last job? ____
4. Why did you leave your last job? ____
5. Why do you think you would be good at this job? ____
6. What do you want to do in ten years? ____

a. I'm interested in this job because I'm good at fixing cars.
b. I want to own my own business.
c. I have a strong work ethic and good people skills.
d. At my last job, I made repairs on houses and operated large machines.
e. Yes. I was a carpenter in Mexico.
f. I left my last job because it was too far from my home.

C Imagine that you are applying for a job. Answer the questions. Then interview your partner.

Job you are applying for: _____

1. Why are you interested in this job? _____

_____

2. Do you have any experience doing this type of work? If yes, please describe your

experience to me. _____

_____

3. What were your responsibilities at your last job? _____

_____

4. Why did you leave your last job? _____

_____

5. Why do you think you would be good at this job? _____

_____

6. What do you want to do in ten years? _____

_____

© Cambridge University Press 2010

Photocopiable

Employment

Worksheet 74 *Electing the U.S. government*

A Read the article. Complete the chart.

The U.S. Government and the Election Process

The U.S. government has three branches: executive, legislative, and judicial. There are three branches so that one branch does not become too powerful.

The president and the vice president form the executive branch of the government. The president is the leader of the country and the military. The vice president becomes president if the president cannot serve. He or she can also vote in the Senate to break a tie. They are both elected, or chosen, for four-year terms. Since 1852, the president has been a member of one of two major political parties: the Democrats or the Republicans. Members of a political party have similar ideas about how to run the government.

The U.S. Senate and House of Representatives are known as Congress. Congress is the legislative branch of the government. Congress makes laws. There are 100 U.S. senators – two from each of the 50 states. There are 435 U.S. representatives, but the number of representatives is different for each state. The number depends on how many people live in each state. Americans elect senators for six-year terms and representatives for two-year terms. U.S. senators and representatives are usually members of the Democratic or Republican parties.

The Supreme Court is the most important part of the judicial branch of the U.S. government. There are nine Supreme Court justices (judges). They review and explain laws passed by Congress and the president. Presidents choose Supreme Court justices, and they have terms for life.

	How many?	Length of term	Job
President	*one*		
Vice president			*becomes president if the president cannot serve; can vote in the Senate to break a tie*
Senators		*six years*	
Representatives	*435*		
Supreme Court justices		*for life*	

B Talk with a partner. Ask and answer the questions.

1. Are there major political parties in your native country? What are they?
2. The president can serve only two four-year terms. Do you think there should be a limit to the number of terms that a president can serve in the government? Why?

© Cambridge University Press 2010   Photocopiable

Worksheet 75 *Jaime registers to vote.*

A Read. Answer the questions.

Jaime lives in New Hampshire. He wants to register to vote. He is looking at a Web site with frequently asked questions (FAQs) about voting.

Voting FAQs (Frequently Asked Questions)
1. **Who can register to vote in New Hampshire?** You must be a U.S. citizen, at least 18 years old on election day, and live in New Hampshire.
2. **How can I register to vote?** Fill out a registration card. You must bring proof of age, citizenship, and a home address.
3. **Where can I register?** You can register to vote at the town or city clerk's office.
4. **What elections can I vote in?** You can vote in city, state, and national elections.

1. How old do you have to be on Election Day to register to vote? _____

2. Where can Jaime register to vote in New Hampshire? _____

3. What elections can Jaime vote in? _____

B Read Jaime's information. Complete the voter registration card.

Jaime Andres Valencia was born on June 2, 1985. He is a U.S. citizen. His address is 3456 Water Street, Concord, NH. His zip code is 03303. His driver's license number is 000456789. Jaime is a Democrat.

Voter Registration Application	**Party Affiliation**
Are you a U.S. citizen? ☐ yes ☐ no _1_	☐ Republican
Will you be 18 years of age on or before Election Day? ☐ yes ☐ no _2_	☐ Democrat ☐ Other _____ _3_

LAST NAME   FIRST NAME   MIDDLE NAME   DATE OF BIRTH
_____ _____ _____   __ __ / __ __ / __ __ __ __
   4   5   6   M M   D   D   Y   Y   Y   Y
                                                7

STREET ADDRESS   CITY   STATE   ZIP CODE
_____ _____   _____ _____
   8   9   10   11

TELEPHONE (optional)   New voters must show an ID
_____   (driver's license or state ID).

SIGN AND DATE THIS CARD   ID#
_____ _____   _____
                                            12

C Talk with a partner. Ask and answer the questions.

1. Did you register to vote in your native country?
2. Is voting different from or similar to voting in the United States?

© Cambridge University Press 2010   Photocopiable

Worksheet 76 Identification cards in the United States

A Read the article. Answer the questions.

Identification Cards in the United States

Although many countries have national identification (ID) cards, the United States does not have one. However, there are many forms of ID in the United States. These include birth certificates, social security cards, driver's licenses, passports, and other documents.

How do people in the United States get these forms of ID? Native-born American citizens are usually issued a birth certificate when they are born in a U.S. hospital. Parents can also request their child's social security card at birth. Driver's licenses are issued at the Department of Motor Vehicles (DMV). Members of the military carry Department of Defense identification cards. U.S. citizens get passports from the post office and other offices when they need to travel to other countries. Some other forms of ID issued by the U.S. government are certificates of U.S. citizenship and naturalization and permanent resident cards.

There are also ID cards issued by state or local government agencies as well as school ID cards, voter registration cards, and Native American tribal ID cards.

---

1. Is there a national ID card in the United States? _____

2. How do you get a U.S. birth certificate? _____

3. Who uses Department of Defense ID cards? _____

4. What are three other documents that show a person's identity in the United States?

_____

B Complete the application form. Use your own information.

STATE ID CARD APPLICATION

Name _____ _____ _____
    First   Middle   Last

Permanent Address _____ _____ _____ _____
           (Street)   (City)   (State)   (Zip)

Home Phone No. _____   Marital Status   Single   Married

Age _____ Date of Birth _____ _____ _____   Place of Birth _____
            (Month) (Day) (Year)

Hair Color _____   Eye Color _____   Height ____ FT ____ IN

Citizenship _____   Employer/School _____

© Cambridge University Press 2010   **Photocopiable**

Worksheet 77 — The local, state, and federal legal system

A Read the article. Complete the chart.

> The judicial system in the United States is made up of two different court systems: the federal (national) court system and the state court system. The U.S. Constitution states that powers of national and state courts will be shared. However, the Constitution gives certain powers to the federal government and the rest of the powers to the states.
>
> The court systems apply and interpret, or explain, the law. The two types of courts hear different cases. The federal court system hears cases in which two different states are represented. It also hears cases involving federal laws, such as taxes and Social Security. State courts hear cases such as family law and property issues. Both federal and state courts hear criminal cases (cases in which crimes were committed).
>
> There are also local (or city) courts. These courts hear cases such as traffic and parking violations. They also hear some criminal cases, such as misdemeanors (less serious crimes).

	Federal courts	State courts	Local courts
What types of court cases do they hear? (list two)	1. *Cases in which two different states are represented.*		
	2.		

B Read the article. Answer the questions.

Legal Assistance for Low-income Americans

> The Legal Services Corporation (LSC) was formed by the United States Congress to provide low-income Americans with legal assistance, or help with legal issues. LSC helps people when they need to go to court. In order to be eligible for, or able to be included in, this program, you must prove that you need financial help.
>
> To find a program near you, you can look in the LSC directory online. Select your state and county from the list on the Web site. When you submit the state and county you are interested in, you will find a list of agencies near you where you can apply for legal assistance. The listings will show the address, phone number, and e-mail address of the program nearest you.

1. What is the Legal Services Corporation? _____

2. Who is eligible to receive legal services from the LSC? _____

3. How can you find an LSC program near you? _____

© Cambridge University Press 2010   Photocopiable

Worksheet **78** *Citizens' responsibilities*

A Read the article. Answer the questions.

Citizens' Responsibilities in the United States

U.S. citizens have the opportunity and responsibility to be involved in their government. The most important right that citizens have is the right to vote. Citizens 18 years old or older have the right to vote and can register at the local driver's license facility or at the office of the election authority. By voting, Americans participate, or have a voice, in government. Their votes decide who will represent them in the government.

Another responsibility of U.S. citizens is to serve on a jury as a juror. This is known as *jury duty*. A jury is a group of people chosen to go to court to determine whether an accusation against another person or institution is true or false. If a person is chosen to be a juror, he or she must go to court and attend the trial for as long as he or she is needed.

All U.S. citizens are expected to obey the local, state, and federal laws of the country. For example, they are expected to pay income taxes and other taxes on time. The last day to send in federal income tax forms is April 15th.

1. What are two responsibilities of U.S. citizens? *voting and serving on a jury*

2. Who has the right to vote in the United States? _____

_____

3. What does it mean to have a voice in government? _____

_____

4. What is jury duty? _____

_____

5. Why is April 15th an important day in the United States? _____

_____

B Read the flyer. Talk with a partner. Ask and answer the questions.

You can have a voice!
Here are some ways you can make a difference:

- Vote.
- Join a community group.
- Call your senator or representative to give your opinion on an issue or law.

- Run for office.
- Write a letter to your local newspaper.

1. What are some ways that U.S. citizens can make a difference in their country?
2. Have you ever done any of these things in this country or your native country?

© Cambridge University Press 2010 Photocopiable

Worksheet 79 · Immigrants' rights and responsibilities

A Read the article. Circle *T* (true) or *F* (false). Correct the false sentences.

Permanent residents in the United States have certain rights and responsibilities. Many of these are the same rights and responsibilities of U.S. citizens. The Civil Rights Act of 1964 states that all people living in the United States have the right to be free from discrimination (being treated differently) based on their race, ethnicity, and country of origin. People in the United States are protected from discrimination by law in the areas of employment, education, health care, and housing, as well as others. Some of the rights of permanent residents in the United States include the right to:
- Live and work anywhere in the country
- Apply to become U.S. citizens
- Request visas for their husband or wife and unmarried children to live in the United States
- Own property in the United States
- Attend public school and college
- Join certain parts of the U.S. Armed Forces (military)

Some of the responsibilities include:
- Obeying all federal and state laws
- Filing federal and state income tax returns
- Registering with the Selective Service (for males between the ages of 18 and 25)

1. Permanent residents cannot live in the state of Hawaii.   T   F

2. Permanent residents can own an apartment building.   T   F

3. Permanent residents can attend public school.   T   F

4. Permanents residents do not have to pay any taxes.   T   F

B Read the article. Answer the questions.

Finding Legal Assistance for Immigration Issues

People in the United States who need help with an immigration issue have the right to hire an immigration lawyer. Residents can check with their local bar association to find a qualified attorney, or lawyer. If the cost of legal fees is an issue, there are some reduced cost and free legal assistance choices. You can find lists of organizations and attorneys in your area that offer reduced-cost or free legal services on the Internet or in a phone book.

1. What can you do if you need help with an immigration issue? _____

_____

2. How can you find a list of attorneys or organizations that will offer their legal

services at a low cost or free to immigrants? _____

_____

© Cambridge University Press 2010   Photocopiable

Worksheet 80 | Our national, state, and local leaders

A Read the article. Match the state leaders with their responsibilities.

Leaders of the Federal and State Government

The U.S. Constitution calls for both a federal government and state governments. The federal government is responsible for issues that affect all Americans. Each state government is responsible for issues that affect the people living in the state. Federal and state governments have executive, legislative, and judicial branches.

In the federal government, the president is the leader of the executive branch. Congress, which includes the Senate and the House of Representatives, makes up the legislative branch. The Supreme Court leads the judicial branch.

In the state government, the governor is the leader of the executive branch. All states have a legislative branch, and most states have a Senate and House of Representatives. Some states use names such as the "General Assembly" or "House of Delegates" instead of "House of Representatives." Each state also has a supreme court that leads the judicial branch.

Most states have a lieutenant governor, a secretary of state, a treasurer, and an attorney general. The lieutenant governor helps the governor lead the state government. The secretary of state maintains official state records and is usually responsible for state elections. The treasurer is the state's banker and decides how the state should invest its money. The attorney general is the state's lawyer and protects the people of the state.

1. lieutenant governor _b_   a. leader of the state executive branch
2. attorney general ____   b. helps the governor lead the state government
3. secretary of state ____   c. the state's banker
4. governor ____   d. the state's lawyer
5. treasurer ____   e. maintains official state records

B Talk with a partner. Use the information in Exercise A. Ask and answer the questions.

1. What is one difference between the federal government and state governments?
2. How are the federal government and your state government similar?
3. Who are some important leaders in your state?
4. What are their jobs?

© Cambridge University Press 2010 **Photocopiable**

Worksheet 81 *The White House and the U.S. Capitol*

A Read the article. Circle the answers.

The White House

The White House is one of the most famous buildings in the world. It is the official residence, or home, of the president of the United States. It was built between 1792 and 1800. It has 132 rooms and has been used as a home by every president since the early 1800s. The White House is divided into several parts. The East Wing contains offices for the First Lady (the president's wife) and her staff. The First Family lives on the second and third floors of the White House. The West Wing includes the president's office and those of his top staff. The president's main office is called the Oval Office.

1. When was the White House built?
   a. since the early 1800s
   b. between 1792 and 1800
   c. before 1792

2. What is the East Wing used for?
   a. the First Lady and her staff
   b. the First Family
   c. the president's office

3. Where does the First Family live?
   a. in the West Wing
   b. in the East Wing
   c. on the second and third floors

4. What is the Oval Office?
   a. the First Lady's office
   b. the president's main office
   c. the White House staff's office

B Read the article. Answer the questions.

The U.S. Capitol

The U.S. Capitol is another important building. It is the meeting place for the U.S. Congress – the Senate and the House of Representatives. They have met at the Capitol for more than 200 years. Construction, or building, of the U.S. Capitol began in 1793. Many things have happened to the building since then – it has been burned and rebuilt, made larger, and restored (made like new). Today, it is a beautiful building that is a symbol of the American people and their government.

1. Who meets at the U.S. Capitol? _____

2. When did construction of the U.S. Capitol begin? _____

3. What is the U.S. Capitol a symbol of? _____

© Cambridge University Press 2010   Photocopiable

Worksheet 82 The Constitution and the Bill of Rights

A Read the conversation. Circle *T* (true) or *F* (false). Correct the false sentences.

Mother Hi, John. What did you learn in school today?

John I learned about the U.S. Constitution.

Mother That's interesting. What did you learn about it?

John I learned that it's the supreme law of the United States. The organization of the U.S. government, or the way it is set up, is based on the Constitution.

Mother Did you find out when it was adopted, or put into use?

John Yes, I did. It was adopted on September 17, 1787, in Philadelphia, Pennsylvania.

Mother Did you learn about any of the amendments, or changes, that have been made to the Constitution?

John Oh, yes. The first ten amendments are known as the Bill of Rights.

Mother What are some of the rights listed in the Bill of Rights?

John Freedom of speech – people are allowed to say or print anything. Freedom of religion – people can practice any religion . . .

Mother Freedom of assembly, people can meet together . . .

John That's right. Those are all in the first amendment.

1. The Bill of Rights is the supreme law of the United States.   T   F

2. The Constitution was adopted on September 15, 1787.   T   F

3. The first ten amendments are known as the Bill of Rights.   T   F

4. Freedom of speech is a right in the Bill of Rights.   T   F

5. The Constitution was adopted in Washington, D.C.   T   F

B Unscramble the letters to make the words in the box.

amendment	Bill of Rights	freedom	religion	United States
assembly	constitution	Philadelphia	speech	

1. hecpse   __ __ __ __ __ __

2. tmanndeem   __ __ __ __ __ __ __ __ __

3. ignirloe   __ __ __ __ __ __ __ __

4. dmoefer   __ __ __ __ __ __ __

5. ttnniicostuo   __ __ __ __ __ __ __ __ __ __ __ __

6. sutindestaet   __ __ __ __ __ __ __ __ __ __ __ __ __

7. bayslmse   __ __ __ __ __ __ __ __

8. rbigthilfols   __ __ __ __ __ __ __ __ __ __ __ __ __

9. adppehlalhii   __ __ __ __ __ __ __ __ __ __ __ __

© Cambridge University Press 2010   Photocopiable

Worksheet 83 · *The American Revolution*

A Read the article. Complete the timeline.

> The American Revolution was a war in which the thirteen original colonies gained independence, or freedom, from England. It all started with the French and Indian War, which lasted from 1756 to 1763. Once the British defeated the French and their American Indian allies, England had control over a lot of North America. England had to spend a lot of money on the war. So the British government decided that the colonists would have to help pay some of these expenses.
>
> To raise money, the British Parliament passed the Stamp Act in 1765. This law made the colonists pay taxes when they bought paper. The colonists were very unhappy about the new taxes. They said that since they were not represented in the British government, they should not have to pay taxes. There was such a big protest against the Stamp Act that the British stopped making them pay it. However, the colonists still had to pay new taxes on items such as sugar and tea. In 1773, a group of protesters from Boston, Massachusetts, threw 342 chests of tea into Boston Harbor as a way of protesting the taxes on tea.
>
> All of these conflicts led to the start of the American Revolution. On July 4, 1776, the Declaration of Independence was signed. It announced the separation of the colonies from the British. This was the beginning of the United States of America.

1756–1763	1765	1773	July 4, 1776
The French and Indian War	_____	_____	_____

B Read the article again. Answer the questions.

1. What was the Stamp Act? _____

2. Why did a group of citizens from Boston throw tea into Boston Harbor in 1773? _____

_____

3. What was the result of the American Revolution? _____

_____

4. What happened on July 4, 1776? _____

_____

C Talk with a partner. Ask and answer the questions.

1. What are some significant wars in your native country's history?
2. Why do you think they happened?

© Cambridge University Press 2010   Photocopiable

Worksheet 84 *George Washington, the nation's first president*

A Read the article. Circle the answers.

George Washington was the first president of the United States of America. He was president from 1789 to 1797. He served for two terms (eight years). His vice president was John Adams, who became the second president of the United States.

Washington was born in Virginia in 1732. He fought for the British in the French and Indian War. At the start of the Revolutionary War between the colonies and the British, Washington was chosen as commander in chief of the American Continental Army (in 1775). And in 1776, the colonists declared their independence from the British.

In 1787, Washington led the Constitutional Convention in Philadelphia, Pennsylvania. At this time the U.S. Constitution (the supreme law of the United States) was written. Washington was elected president of the United States in 1789 and again in 1792. During his presidency, the Bill of Rights, the first ten amendments, or changes, to the Constitution, were written and adopted.

Washington died in 1799 in Mt. Vernon, Virginia. After he died, the nation's capital was moved from Philadelphia, Pennsylvania, to the border of Virginia and Maryland near Washington's home. The new capital was named Washington, District of Columbia (Washington, D.C.), in honor of the first president.

1. What did Washington do before he became president?
   a. He led the Constitutional Convention.
   b. He was vice president.

2. What was written during Washington's presidency?
   a. the Constitution
   b. the Bill of Rights

3. How many times was George Washington elected as president of the United States?
   a. once
   b. twice

4. What happened after Washington's death?
   a. The capital was moved near his home and named after him.
   b. The Bill of Rights was adopted.

B Read the article again. Complete the chart.

Date	Event
	Washington was born in Virginia.
1776	
1787	
	He became president for the first time.
1792	
	George Washington died.

© Cambridge University Press 2010 Photocopiable

Worksheet 85 · Patrick Henry

A Read the conversation. Answer the questions.

Ravi Hi, John. Can you help me with my civics homework?

John Sure. What are you working on?

Ravi I have to give an oral report on Patrick Henry tomorrow.

John OK, what have you already found out about him?

Ravi I learned that Patrick Henry was born in 1736 in Virginia, and that he was famous for being a radical, a person who supports political change.

John That's right. He's a symbol of the American colonists' fight for liberty (freedom).

Ravi Yes. He was a lawyer who fought for liberty and self-government. He helped the colonists to fight for their rights against the British.

John Do you know about his famous speeches?

Ravi No. What are they?

John Well, his most famous speech was when he asked his fellow Virginians to fight against the British. In his famous line, he said, "Give me liberty or give me death."

Ravi That was the beginning of the American Revolution, right?

John That's right.

Ravi Thanks so much for your help, John. I'm going to practice my report now.

John Good luck!

1. When and where was Patrick Henry born? _____

_____

2. What is Patrick Henry a symbol of? _____

_____

3. What was Henry fighting for? _____

_____

4. What did Henry mean when he said, "Give me liberty or give me death"? _____

_____

B Read the article again. Circle *T* (true) or *F* (false). Correct the false sentences.

1736

1. Patrick Henry was born in ~~1739~~.   T   Ⓕ

2. He protested against the way the British treated the French.   T   F

3. He was famous for being a radical.   T   F

4. He served in public office for 20 years.   T   F

5. One of Patrick Henry's most famous speeches includes the line,   T   F
   "Give me liberty or give me death."

© Cambridge University Press 2010   Photocopiable

Worksheet 86 — Thomas Jefferson

A Read the timeline about Thomas Jefferson. Answer the questions.

April 13, 1743	Thomas Jefferson was born.
1776	He wrote the Declaration of Independence.
July 4, 1776	The Declaration of Independence was adopted by the United States at Independence Hall in Philadelphia. It announced the United States' independence from Great Britain. Three rights in the Declaration of Independence are life, liberty, and the pursuit of happiness.
1801	Jefferson became the third president of the United States. He believed in Republicanism, the belief that the main power of a country belongs to the people. He believed in the separation of church and state (government). He also believed in states' rights and a limited federal government, or a government kept to a small size.
July 4, 1826	Jefferson died. He died on the fiftieth anniversary of the Declaration of Independence.

1. Why was the Declaration of Independence important? _____

_____

2. What was one of Jefferson's beliefs? _____

_____

3. What was significant about the day Jefferson died? _____

_____

4. How old was Jefferson when he died? _____

B Complete the puzzle.

DOWN

1. Jefferson believed in the _____ of church and state.
3. Jefferson was _____ in 1743.
4. Jefferson _____ in 1826.

ACROSS

2. A right in the Declaration of Independence is the pursuit of _____ .
4. Jefferson wrote the _____ of Independence.
5. Jefferson was the third _____ of the United States.

© Cambridge University Press 2010   **Photocopiable**

Worksheet **87** *The national anthem and the American flag*

A Read. Find the bolded words.

Francis Scott Key wrote *The Star-Spangled Banner*, our national anthem (national song), during the War of 1812 between the United States and Great Britain. It is about the American flag:

> O say can you see, by the **dawn**'s early light,
> What so proudly we **hailed** at the twilight's last gleaming,
> Whose broad stripes and bright stars through the **perilous** fight
> O'er the **ramparts** we watched were so **gallantly** streaming?
> And the rocket's red **glare**, the bombs bursting in air,
> Gave **proof** through the night that our **flag** was still there,
> O say does that star-spangled **banner** yet wave
> O'er the land of the free and the home of the **brave**?

e	x	y	b	d	r	a	m	p	a	r	t	s	g	a	l	l	a	n	t	l	y
n	v	s	m	b	a	n	n	e	r	q	o	d	k	l	d	a	w	n	g	b	k
p	e	r	i	l	o	u	s	m	z	a	m	i	r	f	l	a	g	o	n	t	m
r	y	v	m	w	g	l	a	r	e	p	v	a	s	k	l	h	a	i	l	e	d
o	e	r	b	r	a	v	e	h	d	e	l	i	m	n	o	k	p	r	o	o	f

B Read the article. Answer the questions.

The American flag is an important symbol in the United States. The colors of the flag are red, white, and blue. Each color represents something. It has been said that red stands for bravery; white stands for purity; and blue stands for justice (being right and fair). There are 13 red and white stripes on the flag. Each stripe symbolizes (stands for) one of the original 13 colonies in the United States. There are also 50 stars on the flag. Each star represents one of the current 50 states in the country.

1. What does each color of the American flag stand for? _____

   _____

2. Why are there 13 stripes on the American flag? _____

   _____

3. What do the stars on the American flag represent? _____

   _____

© Cambridge University Press 2010   Photocopiable

Worksheet 88 *Causes of the Civil War*

A Read the article. Match the words with the meanings.

Causes of the Civil War

What were the causes of the American Civil War? There were several. The war was fought between the northern and southern states. Northerners and southerners disagreed with each other about many things. The biggest disagreement they had was about **slavery** (owning people and forcing them to work). America was an agricultural, or farming, nation, and farmers in the South grew crops like cotton, sugar, and rice. Southern plantation owners wanted slaves to harvest, or gather a lot of crops, quickly. In addition to working on the plantations, slaves also worked in houses.

Many northerners felt that slavery was wrong and should be **abolished**, or ended. People who wanted to end slavery were called **abolitionists**. However, southerners felt that their opinions were not being heard by the government. They threatened to **secede**, or break away, from the United States. They wanted to govern, or be in charge of, themselves.

Abraham Lincoln was elected president of the United States in 1860. He wanted to keep the country united (together), and he was against slavery. Shortly after Lincoln was elected, South Carolina and six other southern states seceded from the nation. They called themselves the **Confederate States of America**. They elected Jefferson Davis as their new president.

On April 12, 1861, the Confederate States of America attacked Fort Sumter in South Carolina. The fort flew the United States flag and was protected by Union (northern) troops. The attack was the start of the fighting between the North and the South in the American Civil War. The war lasted for four years. Men from the South volunteered, or offered, to fight the war to protect the southern way of life. Northern men volunteered because they thought the country should not be divided and that slavery was wrong.

By the end of the war, 620,000 lives had been lost. The northern states won. The country remained united, and slavery was abolished.

1. abolitionists
2. slavery
3. secede
4. Confederate States of America
5. abolished

a. the group of states that seceded from the Union
b. break away
c. people who wanted to end slavery
d. owning people and forcing them to work
e. ended

B Talk with a partner. Answer the questions.

1. What was the biggest disagreement between northerners and southerners?

2. What were the Confederate States of America?

3. Why did the confederate states attack Fort Sumter?

4. What happened at the end of the American Civil War?

© Cambridge University Press 2010   Photocopiable

Worksheet 89 · *The Civil Rights Movement*

A Read the paragraph. Answer the questions.

The Civil Rights Movement began because African Americans were segregated, or kept apart, and treated differently from white Americans. African Americans could not eat or drink at the same places as white Americans. They also could not attend the same schools or ride in the same seats on buses and trains as white Americans.

The Civil Rights Movement began in the early 1950s. One major event was when the U.S. Supreme Court desegregated (stopped segregating) the public schools in 1954. Then, in 1955, Rosa Parks, an African-American woman, stood up against racial discrimination (treating people differently because of their race). In December 1955, she got on a bus after a long day at work. When a white man got on the bus, she was told to stand up so that the white man could sit down. She refused to do so and was arrested.

In 1964, Congress passed the Civil Rights Act. In 1965, the Voting Rights Act was passed. These acts gave all Americans basic rights no matter what their race or gender.

1. Why did the Civil Rights Movement begin? _____

2. Who was Rosa Parks? _____

3. What did the Civil Rights and Voting Rights Acts do? _____

B Read about two civil rights leaders. Check (✔) the box under the correct leader.

Two Americans who were important civil rights leaders were Susan B. Anthony and Martin Luther King, Jr. Susan B. Anthony was a teacher and a women's rights activist. She traveled the country to speak about women's suffrage, or women's right to vote, and the abolition, or ending, of slavery.

Martin Luther King, Jr., was a pastor and civil rights activist. He worked most of his life to gain civil rights for African Americans. He led many nonviolent protests and marches against racial discrimination. He received the Nobel Peace Prize for his work in the Civil Rights Movement in 1964. Today the American people celebrate the national holiday, Martin Luther King Jr. Day, around his birthday in January.

	Anthony	King
1. I was a teacher and women's rights activist.	☐	☐
2. I was a pastor and civil rights activist.	☐	☐
3. I led many nonviolent protests against racial discrimination.	☐	☐
4. I worked for women's right to vote.	☐	☐
5. I spoke about the abolition of slavery.	☐	☐
6. I received the Nobel Peace Prize in 1964.	☐	☐

© Cambridge University Press 2010   Photocopiable

Worksheet 90 | The Statue of Liberty and the Liberty Bell

A Read the article. Circle *T* (true) or *F* (false). Correct the false sentences.

The Statue of Liberty

The Statue of Liberty is an important symbol in the United States. It is located on Liberty Island in New York Harbor. The statue was a gift of friendship from the people of France to the people of the United States. It was given by France to celebrate the centennial (100-year anniversary) of the writing of the Declaration of Independence. The statue was given to the United States to represent the friendship between the two countries that was formed during the American Revolution. It was dedicated to the United States on October 28, 1886. In 1924, it was designated as a national monument. (A monument is something built to remember a time in history.) The Statue of Liberty was restored for its centennial on July 4, 1986.

1. The Statue of Liberty is located in North Carolina.   T   F
2. It was given to the United States by France as a sign of friendship.   T   F
3. It was given ten years after the Declaration of Independence was written.   T   F
4. The statue was designated as a national monument is 1934.   T   F
5. The statue was restored for its centennial on July 4, 1986.   T   F

B Read. Complete the chart.

Frequently Asked Questions (FAQs) About the Liberty Bell

1. **Where is the Liberty Bell located?** In Philadelphia, Pennsylvania
2. **When was it originally cast, or made?** In 1752
3. **Who owns the Liberty Bell?** The city of Philadelphia
4. **Why does the bell have a crack in it?** It cracked the first time it was rung.
5. **Why is the Liberty Bell an important symbol in the United States?** It symbolizes freedom and justice.

Location	Philadelphia, Pennsylvania
Year originally cast	
Owner	
Reason for the crack	
What does it symbolize?	

© Cambridge University Press 2010   Photocopiable

Teacher tips

Worksheet 1 Bring bank deposit and withdrawal slips to class, and show students how to complete them.

Worksheet 2 Locate two housing advertisements with simple abbreviations. Cover text and create information gap exercises. Have students work in pairs, asking and answering questions to complete the missing information. Students can also talk about where to find housing ads.

Worksheet 3 Have pairs of students speak about their experiences with housing problems. Tell them to make up a conversation between Sam and his landlord. This conversation is a follow-up to the one between Sam and Sarah on Worksheet 3.

Worksheet 4 Ask students to brainstorm other emergencies. Put students in pairs. Tell them to role-play calling 911. Make sure they ask for pertinent information, using the conversation on Worksheet 3 as a guide.

Worksheet 5 Ask students to brainstorm any needs or problems at the school or in the program. Write these needs or problems on the board. Ask students what they can do as a class to try to solve some of the problems.

Worksheet 6 Bring in maps of your neighborhood. Put students in small groups. Give each group a copy of the map. Ask students to find important places on their maps. Allow each group 3 minutes to talk about one important place in front of the class, pointing to its location on the map as they speak about it.

Worksheet 7 Ask students to bring something in that represents their culture and native country. Give each student 1 minute to present the item to the class. Have a question-and-answer period in which other students ask questions about the items that students bring to the class.

Worksheet 8 Bring in copies of a driving manual from your local DMV. Ask students to look at the pictures of road signs in the manual. Discuss what each road sign means in class. Check for understanding.

Worksheet 9 Brainstorm ways that adult learners can become successful learners. Write good study strategies on the board. Make a poster of these strategies, and encourage students to use them on a daily basis. If your students have school-aged children, brainstorm ways that they can help their children with their study habits.

Worksheet 10 Ask students to brainstorm a list of other emergencies, and write their responses on the board. Be sure that students understand when they should not call 911, e.g., if their bike or pet is missing.

Worksheet 11 Draw a two-columned chart on the board. Write "emergency" and "nonemergency" as headings in the two columns. Ask students to brainstorm various emergency and nonemergency situations. Ask students what they should do in an emergency situation and in a nonemergency situation.

Worksheet 12 Bring in copies of a local phone book to class. Ask students to look up a page in the book that is similar to the one on Worksheet 12. Ask students to write down the numbers that correspond to the agencies that are listed in this worksheet. Tell students that anybody can call these numbers for help with domestic violence and other problems.

Worksheet 13 Brainstorm the needs of senior citizens with your class. If you have access to a computer lab, ask students to look up services that are available to seniors in your local community. Alternatively, do a search yourself and make copies of the results for your students to look at in class.

Worksheet 14 If you have access to a computer lab, ask students to search for "rights of immigrants in the United States." Ask students if they can find any other rights and responsibilities of immigrants. Ask students if they have had a personal experience going to local agencies that specialize in immigrant services.

Worksheet 15 Bring in pamphlets from local agencies that deal with parenting issues. Ask students with children if they have used the services from these agencies. If you have students with children in your class, invite someone from one of these agencies to speak to your students about their services.

Worksheet 16 Visit the public library with your students. Show them where they can read about recreational activities and cultural events on the bulletin board.

Worksheet 17 Bring in copies of a phone book, or photocopy key pages. Ask students to work in small groups to identify the phone numbers for the local police, fire, parks and recreation departments, etc.

Worksheet 18 Draw two columns on the board. Write the headings "suspicious activity" and "crime" in each of the columns. Ask students if they would like to volunteer any examples of these events that they know about from their lives or from the news.

Worksheet 19 Bring in pamphlets from local health-care agencies in the community. Ask students to form small groups. Give each group a different pamphlet. Tell students to prepare to tell the class about the agency they are reading about. They should include the type of services provided and the eligibility requirements.

Worksheet 20 Ask students if they know how to perform CPR. Bring in pamphlets about first aid and CPR classes in the community. Ask students if they are interested in attending these types of classes in the future.

Worksheet 21 Put students in pairs. Tell them to role-play a conversation between a doctor and a patient. The patient must tell the doctor his / her symptoms, and the doctor will make a diagnosis of the patient.

Worksheet 22 Bring in copies of the local phone book, or make copies of the section listing local pharmacies. Ask students which pharmacies they have gone to. Discuss the locations and hours of these pharmacies.

Worksheet 23 Ask students if they think a typical American diet is healthy and nutritious. Ask students to compare American food with typical food from their native country. Which country's diet is more nutritious?

Worksheet 24 Locate three help-wanted ads from newspapers or the Internet. Create fictional profiles of job candidates. Distribute a copy of the ads and the profiles to small groups. Ask students to write down all of the abbreviations and their meanings. Then ask students to decide which jobs are best for each candidate.

Worksheet 25 Bring in additional pictures of job safety or hazard signs. Ask students to guess what the signs mean and where they would see these signs.

Worksheet 26 If you have any students in your class who work, ask them to tell the rest of the class the expectations their bosses have of them. Ask students to compare employee expectations in the United States to their native countries.

Worksheet 27 Ask students if they know about the history of the first president of the United States. Talk about George Washington and his roles as the first president and commander in chief of the Continental Army.

Worksheet 28 Ask students to brainstorm environmental problems in their community. Ask students what they or others can do to help with these problems. Consider inviting a guest speaker to your class to inform students about recycling opportunities in your area.

Worksheet 29 Ask students if anyone in the class has an ID card from their native country. Ask students to show them to the class, or draw an example on the board. Ask students what other forms of identification they can use in the United States, such as passports and Social Security cards.

Worksheet 30 Ask students to sit in pairs. Ask students to take any change out of their pockets and to tell their partners what kind of coins they have. Partners will listen and make corrections if necessary. Ask students to total the amount of coins they have.

Worksheet 31 Bring to class pictures of the different types of homes featured in the worksheet: apartment, townhouse, condominium, duplex, and mobile home. Ask students what each picture represents.

Worksheet 32 If you have access to a computer lab, ask students to look up www.hud.gov. Ask students to make a list of the different services HUD offers. Alternatively, bring in copies of this Web site for students to look at.

Worksheet 33 Bring to class take-out menus from local restaurants. Ask students to form pairs. Pairs should take turns playing the roles of customer and waiter. The customer places the order, and the waiter calculates the customer's bill.

Worksheet 34 Bring in flyers or brochures about programs at your school or in the neighborhood. Put students into small groups. Have students discuss their educational and career goals. Have students review the flyers and direct questions to the class.

Worksheet 35 Bring in some brochures for different childcare facilities in your area. Ask students to sit in small groups. Tell students to list the positive features of the facility advertised in their brochure.

Worksheet 36 Bring in brochures about Head Start, or ask students to look it up on the Internet. Ask students to list the benefits of this program. What can they / their children gain from Head Start?

Worksheet 37 Have students compare their lists of emergency telephone numbers. Create a class emergency telephone list. Have students put the information into a poster.

Worksheet 38 Bring in a class catalog from your local parks and recreation department. Ask students to look for classes that they or their children might be interested in. Put students in pairs. Ask students to tell their partners about the classes they are interested in and explain why.

Worksheet 39 Ask students if they have any problems in their neighborhoods. Write the problems on the board. Brainstorm ways that students can get help for these problems. Tell students about community services that are available in their communities.

Worksheet 40 Ask students if they volunteer in their children's schools or anywhere else in the community. Tell students about different ways they can help their community and improve their English through volunteering.

Worksheet 41 Bring in flyers from different schools in your area. Include different types of schools, such as magnet, charter, and private schools. Ask students to sit in groups and look at the flyers together. Ask students to rank the schools. Which one is the best? Which one is not so good? Why?

Worksheet 42 If you have access to a computer lab and the Internet, ask students to look up the U.S. Postal Service's Web site (www.usps.com). Tell students to write down the different services that the Postal Service offers. If they do not have access to the Internet, make copies of the home page of this Web site for students to use in class.

Worksheet 43 Ask students to form small groups and share ways they have learned to manage their time. They should decide which time-saving technique is the best or most unusual and then share it with the class.

Worksheet 44 Consider visiting your local library as a class. Ask a librarian to give students a tour so they can learn about different library resources. Encourage students to check books and videos out from the library. Encourage them to check out materials in English to help improve their language skills.

Worksheet 45 Ask students to practice writing letters to their child's teacher about other concerns, such as an absence or illness. Alternatively, have students brainstorm questions that a parent might ask in a parent-teacher conference. They can role-play having a conference with a teacher.

Worksheet 46 Bring in copies of a map of the neighborhood. Have students work in small groups and look up the locations of emergency shelters in the community on the Internet or in phone books. Have students mark off the locations on their maps.

Worksheet 47 Ask students to draw a map of their neighborhood and label local businesses, schools, and bus and train stops. (Have sample maps available.) Then have students exchange maps with a partner. Student A will ask to how to get from one location to another, and then Student B will respond.

Worksheet 48 Have a class discussion about the benefits of public and private health care. Get students to give reasons for and against both types.

Worksheet 49 Bring in flyers from a local health clinic. Ask students to sit in small groups. Tell students to make a list of the services provided by the local health clinic. Discuss different types of doctors and health screenings.

Worksheet 50 Bring to class sample help-wanted ads from the newspaper or Internet. Distribute one ad to each pair of students. Ask students to work together to identify the job requirements. Discuss with students about resources for meeting job requirements.

Worksheet 51   Bring in information about employment-related services. Have students share their questions for the employment counselor from Exercise C with the class.

Worksheet 52   Ask students to write down workers' rights in the United States in list form on the board. Discuss why each of the rights is important for workers.

Worksheet 53   Print out a sample employment application from the Internet. Distribute a blank copy to each student and ask them to complete it with their own information. After students have finished the application, ask them to exchange applications with a partner and check for errors.

Worksheet 54   Ask students which right they believe is most important. Have them come up with three reasons why this right is most important. Have students go around and share this with the class.

Worksheet 55   Ask pairs of students to create a T-chart on poster paper showing the similarities and differences between their native country's system of government and the system of government in the United States. Then ask them to present their charts to class.

Worksheet 56   Ask students to search for the names of the elected officials in their state. Who are the two U.S. senators from their state? Who is the mayor? Who are the representatives? How can they be contacted?

Worksheet 57   Bring in copies of applications for identification cards such as driver's licenses, state ID cards, or passports. Choose a section of the application for students to fill out. Review the data fields so that students understand what goes in each.

Worksheet 58   Before class, prepare a list of five holidays from various cultures. Write the list on the board. Divide students into groups. Instruct each group to select a holiday from a culture with which they are unfamiliar and create a poster explaining that holiday. One student from each group should present the group's poster to the class.

Worksheet 59   Ask students to brainstorm ideas about why it is important to vote. Discuss why they think some people do not vote in the United States and in their native countries.

Worksheet 60   Show students a world map. Ask them to show the city and country that they are from on the map. Then ask them to show the distance from the city and state they live in. Who comes from the farthest place? Who comes from the closest place?

Worksheet 61   Write a few scenarios in which consumers have complaints about specific products. Explain the Consumer Protection Agency to students. Ask students to form pairs. Each pair should then write a complaint letter to the Consumer Protection Agency.

Worksheet 62   Ask students to sit in small groups. Tell them that they are going to plan their own business. They should discuss the type of business, name of the business, how to get money to start the business, and if the type of business they have chosen is appropriate for where they live.

Worksheet 63   Locate several housing ads. To appeal to visual learners, make simple posters about fictional characters and their criteria for an apartment. Ask students to work with a partner to determine which ads the characters should respond to.

Worksheet 64   Distribute copies of a store return policy to students. Return policies can often be found at a store's Web site. Create scenarios based on the store policies.

Worksheet 65   Invite students to brainstorm ideas for what a tenant should do when there is a problem with his or her landlord. Have students work with a partner to prepare a role play between a tenant and a landlord about a problem.

Worksheet 66   After pairs complete Exercise C, ask each pair to share their best money-saving tip with the class. Write their ideas on the board. Assign one student to copy the ideas from the board on a separate list. Type up the "master" list and distribute the tips to the class.

Worksheet 67   Bring copies of local bus and train schedules to class. Students work in pairs to write four to six questions related to getting to and from different stations and how long it takes. Then have student pairs exchange questions. The pairs will then join together to check the answers.

Worksheet 68   Ask students to brainstorm a list of additional suggestions for staying safe on the road. Write students' ideas on the board.

Worksheet 69   Ask students if they or their children attended public or private schools in their native countries. Ask them which schools they would like their children to attend in the United States. Encourage students to tell why they have these preferences.

Worksheet 70   Bring in copies of brochures from different health insurance companies. Ask students to look up what is NOT covered by that insurance company. Tell them to make a list on a piece of paper. Ask them if they think these are fair policies or not.

Worksheet 71   Ask students about substance abuse problems in their native countries. Are they as severe as they are here in the United States? What is done to help people with substance abuse in their native countries?

Worksheet 72   Bring in flyers for a job fair. Have students work in groups to identify the requirements for attending and the kinds of jobs available. Ask students to discuss how they would prepare for a job fair.

Worksheet 73   Reserve time in a computer lab with Internet access. Ask students to search for job interviewing tips. Then ask them to form groups and share what they learned. Afterward, have each group compile a list of interviewing tips. Then ask each group to share tips that it discussed.

Worksheet 74   Ask students to draw a blank chart like the one in Exercise A in their notebooks. Have students work individually to complete the chart with information about government leaders in their native countries. Then ask students to form groups of three to share the information in their charts.

Worksheet 75   Bring in copies of your state's voter registration card. Go over fields and clarify any new terminology. Have students practice filling it out.

Worksheet 76   Ask students if they think it is a good idea for a country to have a national ID card. Tell students to list their reasons. Why do they think the United States does not have a national ID card?

Worksheet 77   Ask students if they have ever gotten traffic tickets or gone to court. Ask them to share their experiences. Ask students if they think the court system or the penal system in the United States is similar to or different from the systems in their native countries.

Worksheet 78   Discuss the rights of everyone living in the United States, such as freedom of speech or assembly. Present scenarios about individuals and have students decide if those individuals were acting within their rights as citizens.

Worksheet 79 Ask students if any of them are applying or have applied to become U.S. citizens or permanent residents. Ask students to share their experiences with the application process with the rest of the class.

Worksheet 80 Have students compose a letter to the governor or to another elected official. Students should edit their letters with a partner. If the class decides to send them, review each letter and ask students to revise their letters based on your comments.

Worksheet 81 Bring in information about Independence Hall and explain that it is another important American landmark. Have students discuss the importance of certain buildings / landmarks in the United States and in their native countries.

Worksheet 82 Bring in copies of the Constitution or the Preamble. Ask students to read the Preamble. Ask students to discuss what they think the Preamble means. Explain difficult terminology.

Worksheet 83 Give students copies of the Declaration of Independence. Highlight the first sentence of the second paragraph ("We hold these truths to be self-evident . . . "). Ask students what they think these words mean. Go over difficult terminology.

Worksheet 84 If you have access to a computer lab, ask students to look up George Washington on the Internet. Tell students to look up interesting facts about him. Ask students to share what they found with the rest of the class.

Worksheet 85 Bring in a recording of Patrick Henry's speech "Give me liberty or give me death." Alternatively, make copies of the speech and read it aloud as students listen and read along with you. Discuss the meaning of the speech.

Worksheet 86 Ask students to talk about famous leaders in their native countries' histories. Encourage them to write the names of the leaders on the board and give a brief explanation about why they were famous.

Worksheet 87 Ask students to talk about their native countries' flags and national anthems. Ask volunteers to draw pictures of their country's flag on the board or to bring in an example of their flag. Ask volunteers to sing part of their national anthem to the class.

Worksheet 88 Ask students to look up an American Civil War map on the Internet or bring in copies of a Civil War map. Ask students to write down which states belonged to the Confederate States of America and which states were part of the United States of America during the Civil War.

Worksheet 89 Ask students to discuss other world leaders who have worked to improve civil rights. Who are / were these leaders? What did they do to improve civil rights in those countries?

Worksheet 90 Ask students if any of them have visited the Statue of Liberty or the Liberty Bell. Encourage students to share their experiences visiting these places with the rest of the class. Encourage students to talk about or bring in pictures of famous landmarks in their native countries.

Answer key

Worksheet 1

A

1. cash
2. a check
3. a credit card
4. an ATM card

B

1. d   3. b   5. c
2. a   4. f   6. e

C

3, 5, 1, 2, 6, 4

Worksheet 2

A

1. d   2. e   3. b   4. a   5. c

B

1. University Place
2. North Park
3. Sunny Gardens
4. North Park
5. Sunny Gardens

C

1. F – University Place has <u>all</u> utilities included.
2. T
3. F – North Park costs <u>$1,250</u> each month.
4. F – University Place has <u>two</u> bathrooms.
5. T

Worksheet 3

A

1. broken
2. jammed
3. leaking

B

The faucet is leaking. / Call a plumber.
The toilet is broken. / Call a plumber.
The electricity isn't working. / Call an electrician.
The lightbulb won't turn on. / Call an electrician.
The window is broken. / Call the landlord.

C

Answers will vary.

Worksheet 4

A

1. 911
2. Someone broke into her house.
3. 678 Maple Drive
4. the police

B

1. Call 911 in an emergency situation.
2. Join a Neighborhood Watch Association.
3. Lock your doors.

C

Answers will vary.

Worksheet 5

A

4, 5, 6, 1, 3, 2

B

Answers will vary.

Worksheet 6

(Order can vary.)

1. Grand Central Station
2. New York Public Library
3. United Nations
4. Empire State Building

B

1. 350 5th Ave., New York, NY 10018
2. $16.61
3. 8:00 a.m.
4. 365

C

Answers will vary.

Worksheet 7

A

Lorena; Mexico; Spanish
Kalifa; Somalia; Somali
Fabio; Brazil; Portuguese
Shen; China; Mandarin
Yuri; Russia; Russian
Diane; the United States; English

B

Answers will vary.

Worksheet 8

A

1. b   2. c   3. a

B

1. b   2. a   3. b   4. a

C

Answers will vary.

Worksheet 9

A

1. Martinez
2. Miguel
3. 03/08/2003
4. Mexico
5. Male
6. 1234 Spring St., Denver, CO
7. 80220
8. (303) 555-6789
9. The Sandbox Preschool
10. Javier Delgado
11. (303) 555-8876

B

1. school
2. name
3. date of birth
4. phone number

Worksheet 10

A

Answers will vary. Suggested answer: A woman fell off a ladder and hit her head.

B

5, 1, 2, 4, 3

C

1. Carol fell off a ladder.
2. Her head hurts.
3. Carol is at home. She lives at 8 Lake Road in Evanston.
4. An ambulance takes people to the hospital.

D

Answers will vary.

Worksheet 11

A

1. It requires immediate action.
2. It is not serious.

B

1. Put your hand in cold water.
2. Call 911 about an accident.
3. Call 911 about a fire.

C

1. nonemergency
2. emergency
3. emergency

D

Answers will vary.

Worksheet 12

A

1. Her husband hits her.
2. It is violence between family members.
3. Call a hotline.
4. They are phone numbers you call for help with problems.
5. She can find them in the telephone book or on the Internet.

B

1. 555-1234   4. 555-9876
2. 555-4545   5. 555-6789
3. 555-3421

Worksheet 13

A

1. b   2. b   3. b   4. a

B

Down

1. volunteers
4. Senior

Across

2. Meals
3. utility
5. Medicare

Worksheet 14

A

1. F – Permanent residents <u>can</u> work in the United States.
2. F – Permanent residents have to pay income taxes.
3. T
4. T

B

1. responsibilities
2. taxes
3. Selective Service
4. citizen

C

Answers will vary.

Worksheet 15

A

1. c   2. e   3. a   4. b   5. d

B

1. consequences
2. family literacy classes
3. progress

C

Answers will vary.

Worksheet 16

A

1. *Romeo and Juliet*
2. free
3. 7 p.m.
4. Jacobs Park
5. a blanket or chair and a picnic dinner
6. 555-6432

B

family arts festival, Saturday, free; film festival, Saturday, $5; art museum, Sunday, free

Worksheet 17

A

1. 555-5432   5. 555-3412
2. 555-7878   6. 555-9873
3. 555-3321   7. 555-3589
4. 555-0863

B

Answers will vary.

Worksheet 18

A

1. Smith
2. John
3. Yes
4. Man with long brown hair and a tattoo
5. 5'8"
6. 150 lbs
7. brown
8. pickup truck
9. red
10. AGD789
11. I saw a broken window. Then I saw a man leave a neighbor's house and get in a car.

B

1. crime
2. suspicious activity
3. crime
4. suspicious activity
5. suspicious activity
6. crime

Worksheet 19

A

1. c   2. a   3. d   4. b

B

1. what you can afford
2. yes
3. yes
4. yes

Worksheet 20

A

1. c
2. a
3. b

B

1. b   2. c   3. a

C

1. T
2. F – For small burns, <u>do not</u> use ice.
3. F – <u>Do not</u> cover the burn with fluffy cotton.

Worksheet 21

A

1. b   2. a   3. a   4. b

B

1. 555-8909
2. Freedom Health Center
3. 555-6543
4. 555-1234

Worksheet 22

A

1. a   2. b   3. b   4. a

B

1. She has a cold.
2. cold medicine
3. two tablets every 4 hours
4. Follow the instructions on the label.

Worksheet 23

A

1. Fast food like hamburgers and hot dogs.
2. She suggests he eat more salads and pasta.
3. People should eat grains, vegetables, fruits, and milk products.

B

1. vegetable
2. milk
3. grain
4. fruit

C

Answers will vary.

Worksheet 24

A

1. d   2. e   3. f   4. c   5. a   6. b

B

1. b   2. a   3. c   4. c

C

Answers will vary.

Worksheet 25

A

1. e   2. d   3. a   4. c   5. b

B

1. hairnet
2. hard hat
3. safety goggles
4. warnings
5. fire extinguisher

Worksheet 26

A

(Answers can vary.)

1. He works hard and follows all the rules at his job.
2. He arrives at work on time.
3. He does all the work he needs to do.

4. He is friendly.
5. He works well with others.
6. He is dependable and responsible.
7. He always looks neat and wears a clean uniform.

B

```
d i h l a t i l a o r z l l r y q m s l
n l j d t r e s p o n s i b l e y n o v
y i c d i k l g g g y d k w m i o d t y
g s t v r e o i r b h w w t s j t p w c
a u j n x c f r i e n d l y q s r a z l
c k n d d j z n s a c v l g h z s h u g
e h k s u u q w t o d e p e n d a b l e
h p e o b y k e i c y k u u t d n m a i
b s d h a r d w o r k i n g u p k h a c
q d u g q z t b l p q p f h p m t h i j
```

C

Answers will vary.

Worksheet 27

A

  1. a   2. d   3. b   4. c

B

Answers will vary.

Worksheet 28

A

  1. b   2. c   3. a

B

Across

  1. recycle
  4. pollution
  5. reuse

Down

  2. environment
  3. water

C

Answers will vary.

Worksheet 29

A

  1. b   2. a   3. a   4. b

B

  1. Gomes
  2. Roxana
  3. Isela
  4. 08/22/1985
  5. 2456 Pine Street
  6. Sarasota
  7. FL
  8. 34230
  9. Brown
  10. Brown
  11. 5'3"
  12. 105 pounds

Worksheet 30

A

  1. a five-dollar bill
  2. a quarter
  3. a dime

4. a penny
5. a one-dollar bill
6. a nickel

B

1. b 2. e 3. d 4. f 5. a 6. c

C

11¢, $1.05, $5.25, $6.01, $5.15
one dollar and twenty-five cents, $6.95, two dollars and fifty cents, $10.20, twelve dollars, $15

Worksheet 31

A

    Sue rents an <u>apartment</u> now, but she wants to buy a home. She doesn't know what kind of home she should buy. She is married, and she has three children. She and her husband looked at a <u>townhouse</u> in the city, a <u>condominium</u> in a large building, a <u>mobile home</u>, and a <u>duplex</u>. Her husband likes the <u>mobile home</u> because it can move easily to different places. Sue prefers the <u>duplex</u>. She likes the separate entrance and the neighborhood where it is located.

B

1. d 2. a 3. c 4. e 5. b

C

Answers will vary.

Worksheet 32

A

  1. It can help you get a mortgage and know your rights.
  2. It can help people get a reduced rent by offering subsidized housing and vouchers.
  3. It helps the homeless find housing, food, and job skills.

B

1. f 2. d 3. e 4. b 5. a 6. c

C

Answers will vary.

Worksheet 33

A

1. a 2. c 3. b 4. b

B

  1. meat, eggs, dairy products, and beans
  2. fruits and vegetables
  3. Answers will vary.

Worksheet 34

A

adult school, community college, and Regional Occupational Programs
English, job training, and computer classes
talk to your school's admission office and search in the phone book or on the Internet

B

  1. Fall
  2. Silvio
  3. Rivas
  4. 123 Lafayette Ave.
  5. Bloomfield
  6. NJ
  7. 07003
  8. (973) 555-1980
  9. May
  10. 14
  11. 1969
  12. Colombia
  13. Spanish
  14. auto mechanics

Worksheet 35

A

  1. Little Angels Day Care
  2. five
  3. all ages

B

yes, no, no, no, no

C

Answers will vary.

Worksheet 36

A

  1. a 2. b 3. a 4. a

B

  1. School Breakfast
  2. food
  3. Low-income
  4. Homeless, migrant

Worksheet 37

A

  1. F – You should stay <u>calm</u> when you call 911 about an emergency.
  2. T
  3. T
  4. F – You should follow all instructions the 911 operator gives you.

B

  1. Her house is on fire.
  2. her address
  3. the fire department

C

Answers will vary.

Worksheet 38

A

1. You'll learn new skills, make new friends, and have a healthy lifestyle.
2. $50 for five lessons
3. at West Gym

B

1. no
2. new skills
3. police officers
4. It's free.
5. They will have a more interesting and healthy lifestyle.

C

Answers will vary.

Worksheet 39

A

1. a   2. b   3. b   4. a

B

1. yes
2. 911
3. 555-CITY

C

Answers will vary.

Worksheet 40

A

1. Answers will vary.
2. Drum teacher and volunteer at school
3. Habitat for Humanity, drum teacher

B

May 17th, 9:00 a.m., Larry McKenna, 12:15 p.m., 3 hours 15 minutes
May 19th, 4 p.m., Larry McKenna, 7 p.m., 3 hours

Worksheet 41

A

Day care: younger than 3
Preschool: 2½ or 3
Elementary school: 5–10
Junior high school: 11–14
High school: 14–18
Community college or university: 18 and up
Vocational school: high school and up
Adult education: adults

B

Answers may vary.

C

Answers will vary.

Worksheet 42

A

1. b   2. a   3. a   4. b

B

1. b   2. c   3. d   4. a   5. e

C

Answers will vary.

Worksheet 43

A

Mon., January 2: 8:00 p.m., Mr. Gonzalez, Neighborhood Watch meeting
Tues., January 3: 4:00 p.m. to 5:00 p.m., Maria, ballet lessons
Wed., January 4: 5:00 p.m. to 7:00 p.m., Patricia, soccer practice
Thurs., January 5: 4:00 p.m. to 5:00 p.m., Maria, ballet lessons
Fri., January 6: 6:00 p.m., Arturo, hockey game
Sat., January 7: 9:00 p.m., Mr. and Mrs. Gonzalez, concert at the community center

B

Answers will vary.

C

Answers will vary.

Worksheet 44

A

1. T
2. F – You can check out up to 25 items at one time.
3. T
4. F – You will get your library card from the librarian.
5. T
6. T

B

Answers will vary.

C

Answers will vary.

Worksheet 45

A

1. a   2. b   3. a   4. a

B

Answers will vary.

Worksheet 46

A

1. people who lose their homes in a natural disaster
2. the American Red Cross and the Salvation Army
3. They have a lot of hurricanes.
4. so they can be prepared for a hurricane

B

1. b   2. a   3. a   4. b

C

Answers will vary.

Worksheet 47

A

1. north
2. northeast
3. southeast
4. southwest
5. northwest

B

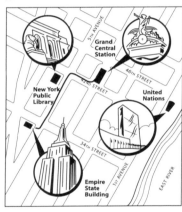

C

Answers will vary.

Worksheet 48

A

1. Medicare: U.S. citizens and residents 65 or older
2. Medicaid: low-income people in certain categories
3. State Children's Health Insurance Program: low-income children
4. Veterans Administration: veterans and their families

B

1. c   2. e   3. d   4. b   5. a

C

Answers will vary.

Worksheet 49

A

1. their immunization records
2. the public health clinic

3. on Main Street
4. shots and prenatal care

B

1. 445 N. Main St., Denver, CO 80220
2. immunizations, prenatal care, pediatric checkups
3. checkups for kids

C

Answers will vary.

Worksheet 50

A

1. You can find ads for jobs in the Classified section of a newspaper under "Employment," on the Internet, or on bulletin boards in your community. You can also ask your friends if they know about any job openings.
2. Answers will vary.

B

1. F – Betty's Coffee Shop is looking for a cook.
2. T
3. F – Experience is necessary for the auto mechanic job.
4. F – You don't need experience to work at Betty's Coffee Shop.
5. F – Call 555-9876 if you want to work at University Hospital.
6. T
7. F – Betty's Coffee Shop needs someone to work Monday through Thursday.
8. T

C

Answers will vary.

Worksheet 51

A

1. They can help you find a new job.
2. It's a paper with information about your work experience.
3. You can look in the newspaper and online.
4. You can practice with a friend.

B

1. He worked at a day-care center.
2. He's friendly and he likes working with children.

C

Answers will vary.

Worksheet 52

A

1. minimum wage
2. overtime

3. disability
4. discrimination

B

1. b   2. a

Worksheet 53

A

1. Miguel
2. Armando
3. Vicente
4. 21000 NW 15th Street, Miami, FL 33179
5. (773) 555-9124
6. 000-456-7890
7. cook
8. 40
9. yes
10. full time
11. immediately
12. Jaime Mora
13. 515 Calle Azul, Nogales, Sonora, Mexico
14. August 2006
15. February 2009
16. cooked different kinds of American food
17. moved to the United States with my family
18. yes

Worksheet 54

A

1. F – The Bill of Rights is the first ten amendments to the U.S. Constitution
2. T
3. F – The fifth amendment states that a person can't be tried twice for the same crime.
4. T
5. T

B

1. People can practice any religion they want.
2. People can say or print what they want.
3. You can meet peacefully with a group of people.

C

Answers will vary.

Worksheet 55

A

1. b   3. b   5. c   7. c
2. c   4. c   6. a   8. b

B

Answers will vary.

Worksheet 56

A

1. Her daughter's teacher lost her job.
2. She could contact the governor.
3. She can use the Internet.

B

1. F – Rita is concerned about her daughter's education.
2. T
3. F – The school will not have art and music teachers next year.
4. T
5. T

C

Answers will vary.

Worksheet 57

A

DOB: 09-15-58
Expires: 01-01-13
Name: Jane Mason
Street Address: 960 Water Street
City, state, zip: Chicago, IL 60611
5'3"
110 lbs
brown eyes

B

1. b   2. b   3. c   4. a

Worksheet 58

A

1. Martin Luther King Jr. Day: People remember Martin Luther King, Jr., for his peaceful fight for equal rights for all Americans.
2. Presidents' Day: People celebrate the first president, George Washington, and the sixteenth president, Abraham Lincoln.
3. Memorial Day: People remember soldiers who died in military service.
4. July 4th: This is the birthday of the United States.
5. Labor Day: Americans celebrate all workers.
6. Columbus Day: Americans remember Christopher Columbus.
7. Veterans Day: We remember people in the military.
8. Thanksgiving: Family and friends get together and have a large dinner.

Worksheet 59

A

1. It gives you a voice.
2. Citizens who are 18 or older
3. Democratic and Republican parties
4. People vote for candidates from their political parties.
5. in November

B

Across

1. Election
5. Democratic
6. primary

Down

2. eighteen
3. vote
4. candidates

Worksheet 60

A

Answers will vary.

B

Answers will vary.

C

Canada, the United States, Mexico, Atlantic, Pacific

Worksheet 61

A

1. F – Writing a letter of complaint is one way to deal with <u>dissatisfaction</u> over a product or service.
2. F – Send <u>a copy of</u> the original receipt of the product you bought with your letter of complaint.
3. T
4. T
5. F – It is necessary to keep a copy of everything you send.

B

Answers may vary.
Dear Mr. Smith:
    I purchased a set of dinner plates from your company on January 2, 2009 <u>online</u>. When the plates arrived in the mail, many of them were broken. <u>The model number was xx0089, and the serial number was 3345. I am including a copy of the receipt.</u> I am very upset and will not buy anything from your company again. <u>I would like a new set of dinner plates.</u>

Sincerely,
Peter Johnson
<u>(703) 555-0912</u>
<u>923 W. Main St.</u>
<u>Southboro, MA 01662</u>

Worksheet 62

A

8, 4, 3, 1, 5, 7, 2, 6

B

1. b   2. c   3. d   4. a

C

Answers will vary.

Worksheet 63

A

1. landlord
2. tenants
3. lease
4. security deposit
5. refunded

B

1. John Marks
2. Sarah Smith
3. May 1, 2009
4. April 30, 2010
5. $400
6. $800
7. first
8. electricity
9. water

Worksheet 64

A

1. F – The TV has a guarantee to last for <u>two</u> years.
2. F – The extended warranty is good for <u>one year</u> after the guarantee expires.
3. T
4. F – Jon is sure that the store will refund his money or <u>exchange his TV for a new one</u>.

B

1. receipt
2. guarantee
3. warranty
4. refund
5. exchange

Worksheet 65

A

1. d   2. c   3. b   4. a

B

1. A tenant should tell the landlord if there is a problem with the property.
2. A tenant should give the landlord advance notice before moving out.
3. A landlord can enter a tenant's home without giving advance notice in an emergency.
4. If a tenant does not pay rent, the landlord can evict the tenant.
5. A landlord can evict a tenant if the tenant does not pay rent; the tenant damages the property; the lease expires, and the tenant does not leave; or the tenant does not do the things he or she agreed to do in the lease.

Worksheet 66

A

1. e   2. d   3. b   4. a   5. c

B

1. $2,500 per month
2. $2,675
3. $175
4. $225

Worksheet 67

A

1. Bus C
2. 8:16 a.m.
3. Bus B
4. one hour and 6 minutes
5. 12 minutes

B

1. Walk north on N. Michigan Ave. Then walk west on W. Randolph St.
2. Walk east on W. Randolph St. Then walk north on N. Michigan Ave. to the John Hancock Observatory.
3. Walk south on N. Michigan Ave. Walk east on E. Chicago Ave.
4. Walk west on E. Chicago Ave. Walk south on N. Michigan Ave. Walk west on W. Randolph St.

Worksheet 68

A

1. the driver and all passengers
2. get a lot of rest
3. take medicine or drink alcohol
4. eat, drink, or talk on the phone
5. stays aware of what is happening on the road
6. every two hours
7. by planning your driving route, bringing directions, and allowing plenty of time for driving

B

1. b   2. d   3. a   4. c

Worksheet 69

A

1. He's in middle school in the 7th grade.
2. He will attend a community college and get an Associate's Degree.
3. A school district is a certain area of a city or town.
4. They make decisions about the schools in their district.

B

Answers will vary.

C

Answers will vary.

Worksheet 70

A

1. Her health insurance company won't pay for her son's medication.
2. Call the insurance company.
3. On the back of the insurance card.

B

1. b   2. a   3. a   4. b

Worksheet 71

A

1. b   2. d   3. e   4. c   5. a

B

1. She's worried that her friend might have an addiction problem.
2. She drinks a lot of alcohol, and she forgets to do important things.
3. He suggests that Ana should talk to a substance abuse counselor.

C

Answers will vary.

Worksheet 72

A

1. F – The job fair is on March <u>12</u>, 2010.
2. F – <u>Forty</u>-five employers will be at the job fair.
3. T
4. F – Call 239-555-75<u>90</u> to register.
5. F – Twenty-year-olds <u>cannot</u> come to the job fair. <u>You must be 21 or older</u>.
6. T

B

1. assistants
2. fill out

3. experience
4. train
5. night

Worksheet 73

A

Answers will vary.

B

1. e   3. d   5. c
2. a   4. f   6. b

C

Answers will vary.

Worksheet 74

A

President: one / four years / leader of the country and the military
Vice President: one / four years / becomes president if the president cannot serve; can vote in the Senate to break a tie
Senators: 100 / six years / make laws
Representatives: 435 / two years / make laws
Supreme Court justices: 9 / for life / review and explain laws passed by Congress and the president

B

Answers will vary.

Worksheet 75

A

1. 18
2. at the town or city clerk's office
3. city, state, and national elections

B

1. yes
2. yes
3. Democrat
4. Valencia
5. Jaime
6. Andres
7. 06/02/1985
8. 3456 Water Street
9. Concord
10. NH
11. 03303
12. 000456789

C

Answers will vary.

Worksheet 76

A

1. no
2. It's issued when you are born in a U.S. hospital.
3. members of the military
4. driver's license, social security card, and passport

B

Answers will vary.

Worksheet 77

A

Federal courts: 1. Cases in which two different states are represented; 2. Cases involving federal laws; 3. criminal cases (list two)
State courts: 1. family law; 2. property issues; 3. criminal cases (list two)
Local courts:
    1. traffic and parking violations;
    2. misdemeanor criminal cases

B

1. It provides legal assistance to low-income Americans.
2. Anyone who can prove that they need financial help.
3. Look in the LSC directory online to find the address, phone number, and e-mail address.

Worksheet 78

A

1. voting and serving on a jury
2. Citizens 18 years or older are allowed to vote.
3. It means you participate in government.
4. It is a responsibility for U.S. citizens to serve on a jury to determine whether an accusation against another person or institution is true or false.
5. It is the last day to send in federal income tax forms.

B

1. U.S. citizens can vote, join a community group, call their senator or representative to give their opinion on an issue or law, run for office, or write a letter to their local newspaper.
2. Answers will vary.

Worksheet 79

A

1. F – Permanent residents <u>can live anywhere in the country</u>.
2. T
3. T
4. F – Permanent residents <u>have to</u> pay taxes.

B

1. You can hire an immigration lawyer.
2. You can look on the Internet or in a phone book.

Worksheet 80

A

1. b 2. d 3. e 4. a 5. c

B

1. The federal government is responsible for issues that affect all Americans. The state government is responsible for issues that affect state residents.
2. Both have executive, legislative, and judicial branches.
3. Answers will vary.
4. Answers will vary.

Worksheet 81

A

1. b 2. a 3. c 4. b

B

1. the U.S. Congress
2. in 1793
3. the American people and their government

Worksheet 82

A

1. F – The <u>Constitution</u> is the supreme law of the United States.
2. F – The Constitution was adopted on September <u>17</u>, 1787.
3. T
4. T
5. F – The Constitution was adopted in <u>Philadelphia</u>, <u>Pennsylvania</u>.

B

1. speech
2. amendment
3. religion
4. freedom
5. Constitution
6. United States
7. assembly
8. Bill of Rights
9. Philadelphia

Worksheet 83

A

1754–1763: The French and Indian War
1765: Stamp Act
1773: tea thrown in Boston Harbor
July 4, 1776: the Declaration of Independence was signed

B

1. a tax on paper
2. to protest the taxes on tea
3. the colonies separated from the British
4. The Declaration of Independence was signed.

C

Answers will vary.

Worksheet 84

A

1. a 2. b 3. b 4. a

B

1732 – Washington was born in Virginia.
1776 – The colonists declared their independence.
1787 – Washington led the Constitutional Convention.
1789 – He became president for the first time.
1792 – He was elected again.
1799 – George Washington died.

Worksheet 85

A

1. in 1736, in Virginia
2. the American colonists' fight for liberty
3. liberty and self-government
4. He wanted to live as a free man.

B

1. F – Patrick Henry was born in <u>1736</u>.
2. F – He protested the way the British treated the <u>colonists</u>.
3. T
4. F – <u>He was a lawyer</u>.
5. T

Worksheet 86

A

1. It announced the United States' independence from Great Britain.
2. Republicanism, the separation of church and state, states' rights, and limited federal government (list one)
3. It was the fiftieth anniversary of the Declaration of Independence.
4. 83

B

Down

1. separation
3. born
4. died

Across

2. happiness
4. Declaration
5. president

Worksheet 87

A

B

1. red for bravery, white for purity, blue for justice
2. The thirteen stripes represent the thirteen colonies.
3. The stars represent the states.

Worksheet 88

A

1. c 2. d 3. b 4. a 5. e

B

1. slavery
2. the states that broke away
3. It flew the U.S. flag and was protected by Union troops.
4. The country remained united.

Worksheet 89

A

1. because African Americans were segregated and treated differently from white Americans
2. She was an African-American woman who stood up against discrimination.
3. They gave all Americans basic rights.

B

1. Anthony
2. King
3. King
4. Anthony
5. Anthony
6. King

Worksheet 90

A

1. F – The Statue of Liberty is located in <u>New York Harbor</u>.
2. T
3. F – It was given <u>100 years</u> after the Declaration of Independence was written.
4. F – The statue was designated as a national monument in <u>1924</u>.
5. T

B

Location: Philadelphia, Pennsylvania
Year originally cast: 1752
Owner: the city of Philadelphia
Reason for the crack: It cracked the first time it was rung.
What does it symbolize? freedom and justice